Library of
Davidson College

THE LENINIST RESPONSE
TO NATIONAL DEPENDENCY

RESEARCH SERIES NO. 37

The Leninist Response to National Dependency

Kenneth Jowitt

INSTITUTE OF INTERNATIONAL STUDIES
University of California
Berkeley

International Standard Book Number 0-87725-137-1

Library of Congress Card Number 78-620061

© 1978 by the Regents of the University of California

To Rebecca and Cullen

CONTENTS

Acknowledgements   x

I. INTRODUCTION   1

II. STATUS SOCIETIES   6

III. NATIONAL DEPENDENCY IN A PEASANT SOCIETY   22

IV. THE LENINIST RESPONSE   34

V. COLLECTIVIZATION   63
    "Familialism" in Communist Countries: A Conjecture   69

VI. COMBINED SUBSTITUTION   74

ACKNOWLEDGEMENTS

This work is informed by concerns, themes, and perspectives that I have dealt with in a number of earlier pieces on revolution, the conception of time and development in Leninist regimes, political culture, the developmental history of Leninist regimes, their international organization, and the comparison of Third World and Leninist regimes. In a year of study provided by a generous grant from the American Council of Learned Societies, I have tried to add to, sharpen, and elaborate upon my ideas. I have benefited from the comments of a number of departmental colleagues such as John Bryan Starr and Gail Lapidus. In addition, I had occasion to discuss this work with members of the Department of Political Science at the University of California, San Diego, for which I thank David Laitin and his colleagues. Professor Melvin Croan provided a highly useful critical review of the work, and I wish to thank him for his criticism and interest. Finally, my good friend and colleague Robert Price maintained his unbroken record of enthusiasm for and critical scrutiny of my work, for which I thank him.

Bojana Ristich has helped me present a large number of themes and arguments in a relatively small space in what I hope is an easily readable fashion. Special thanks to her and the Institute of International Studies at Berkeley.

K. J.

Berkeley, California

I

INTRODUCTION

An outstanding characteristic of studies of Communist regimes is the relative absence of any treatment of the pre-Communist phase; where such treatment does exist, the handling of the pre-Communist and Communist periods is markedly compartmentalized. There are at least two reasons for this. First, Communist totalitarianism was seen as totally discrepant with the existing social and cultural features. Such a view was integrally related to the imposed quality of Communist (Leninist) rule in many cases. Second and most important, none of the analyses that guide research in the field of Communist studies has adequately examined the ways in which Leninist organization relates the status features of a peasant society to the organization of society around impersonal (in our terms class or modern) norms of social action. Yet it is precisely in this area that the distinctive quality of Leninist organization as a response to the "arrested development" of dependent societies can be isolated.

Almost without exception, studies of social change are informed by a distinction between the general and the particular. On the one hand, employed without modification, an emphasis on the "general" produces analyses that fail to adequately appreciate the innovative quality of particular institutional solutions to general developmental problems, and it often confuses specific cases with a general type (e.g., the tendency to see English liberal capitalism as coterminous with modernity). On the other hand, those operating with an emphasis on the "particular" typically discover uniqueness where it does not exist.

One can find instances in both the political and intellectual spheres of this either-or approach. A striking instance of the general over the particular in the political sphere is the Romanian scholar Dobrogeanu-Gherea's notion that because Romania was in the orbit of the capitalist and soon to become socialist West, it would over time and with some socialist education itself become socialist. In contrast, Codreanu's Iron Guard movement was a striking assertion of the particular quality of Romanian life—a uniqueness that had to be protected from the general developments of a Western/alien nature that were threatening it.

In the intellectual sphere the tendency to reify an ideal-typical distinction and apply it directly to institutional development has been brilliantly corrected by Alexander Gerschenkron with his concept of historical substitution.[1] Taking the *general* notion of backwardness, Gerschenkron developed a challenge-response pattern that on the basis of several empirically based indicators enabled him to predict and explain the *particular institutional form* industrialization would take in a country.

Lenin did politically what Gerschenkron did analytically. In opposition both to the Marxists—who argued that the general laws of history plus some socialist electoral propaganda would produce socialism—and to the "peasant-populists"—who stressed the exceptional and unique quality of each peasant society—Lenin, with his "party of a new type," offered a Gerschenkronian solution to the challenge of creating a class form of organization in a non-Western peasant society.

To grasp the novelty of Leninist organization and strategy, it is necessary first to appreciate the defining features of a peasant society, and a readily available means of doing so is by exploring the notion of dependency.[2]

Dependency is not a post-World War II phenomenon. During the late nineteenth and early twentieth centuries, Latin American and East European social organization and political development were comparable in many respects to contemporary Third World patterns. As in the Third World today, three characteristics dominated the social and political reality of an East European country like Romania. First, there was a striking gap between the social elite

---

[1] Alexander Gerschenkron, "Economic Backwardness in Historical Perspective," in *Economic Backwardness in Historical Perspective*, ed. Alexander Gerschenkron (Cambridge, Mass.: Belknap Press, 1966), pp. 5-31. In the same volume see A. Gerschenkron, "The Approach to European Industrialization: A Postscript," pp. 353-67.

[2] The terms (national) dependency and neocolonialism are used almost interchangeably in the literature, even though strictly conceived, they do not refer to identical phenomena. I use the term dependency because I wish to include countries that may never have experienced colonialism.

and the peasantry—what Dobrogeanu-Gherea termed "the abyss between urban and rural Romania."[3] One contemporary Western scholar has even suggested that "in no other European country of the interwar era was the moral and psychological chasm between the oligarchic, bureaucratic elite and the lower classes as wide and as deep."[4]

Second, there was—what in the last several decades has been a common occurrence—the mechanical transfer of liberal institutional facades from the West.[5] The transfer was accompanied by a quasi-magical view of the power and character of these institutions. Referring to the enthusiasts of Western modernization in mid-nineteenth century Romania, Dobrogeanu-Gherea noted that "[Western] political and . . . social institutions appeared to them as a kind of civilized dress, which by replacing the oriental style transformed [Romania] *ipso facto* from oriental to civilized."[6] He went on to observe that underneath the Western "top hat and tails" Balkan culture and social relations continued to thrive (*"să trăească foarte bine şi frumos"*). Almost all Romanian analysts were sensitive to the discrepancy between the definition and operation of institutions "imported" from the West.[7] In their analyses of this discrepancy some, such as Dobrogeanu-Gherea, anticipated many of the arguments about "prismatic" society, "arrested development," and the "development of underdevelopment" set forth by Riggs, Tucker, and radical political economists.[8]

[3] C. Dobrogeanu-Gherea, *Neoiobăgia* [Neo-serfdom] (Bucharest: Editura Librăriei SOCEC & Comp., 1910), p. 5.

[4] Joseph Rothschild, *East Central Europe Between the Two World Wars* (Seattle and London: University of Washington Press, 1974), p. 321.

[5] More recently Leninist institutional facades have been mechanically transferred to African regimes such as Benin and Congo-Brazzaville.

[6] Dobrogeanu-Gherea, *Neoiobăgia*, pp. 1-2.

[7] In his *Istoria civilizaţiei Române moderne* (Bucharest: Editura Stiinţifică, 1972), Eugen Lovinescu noted that the point of departure for Romanian analysts was the "process of importing all the forms of Western civilization with the accompanying contrast between formal character and effective operation" (p. 478).

[8] On "prismatism," see Fred W. Riggs, "The Theory of Developing Polities," in F. Riggs, *Administration in Developing Countries* (Boston: Houghton Mifflin, 1964), pp. 449-67; on "arrested development," see Robert C. Tucker, *The Marxian Revolutionary Idea* (New York: W. W. Norton, 1969), pp. 112-19; and on "the development of underdevelopment," see Colin Leys, *Underdevelopment in Kenya: The Political Economy of Neo-Colonialism* (Berkeley and Los Angeles: University of California Press, 1974), pp. 1-27.

Finally, during this period Romania was seen by its intellectual and political leaders as suffering from multiple dependencies on the West. These dependencies (economic, cultural, political, and military) were not seen simply as the reflection of Romania's relative weakness as a small power, but rather as reflecting and reinforcing the country's social malintegration. The arguments offered by Radulescu-Motru about the confining effects of "neocolonial" cultural-economic definitions on Romania could easily be interchanged with those made by Colin Leys recently in his work on contemporary Kenya. In both cases a situation of "dependence" is related to the ability of an external power(s) to control the definition of appropriate economic institutional behavior—an ability that is integrally related to the external power's status as an authoritative ideological-cultural referent for the local elite. In Radulescu-Motru's words, "[Western] civilization has in truth a great role to play; it is one of the many tentacles of the powerful states."[9]

Interestingly enough, this dependency syndrome of social malintegration, institutional formalism (or prismatism), and multiple dependencies was approached by Romanian (and Western) analysts from much the same perspective as is employed today by students of Third World countries. Very early on in their attempts to come to grips with the quality of social organization and development in Romania, Romanian intellectuals began to argue along *international political economy* lines. Dobrogeanu-Gherea did so most dramatically with his image of backward countries entering into the orbit of advanced capitalist countries and "having their entire life, development, and social movement determined by the development of the more advanced countries."[10] He referred to a small backward country like Romania as a "district" of a more advanced Western Europe.[11]

The international political economy approach has merit as a corrective to perspectives that emphasize an "autarchic" view of national development and neglect the systemic and strategic influence of *international* political and economic structures. Similarly, it has demonstrated its utility as a corrective to perspectives that fail to systematically relate political and economic considerations. How-

[9] C. Radulescu-Motru, *Cultura romana şi politicianismul* (Bucharest, 1936), p. 176.

[10] C. Dobrogeanu-Gherea, "Post-scriptum sau cuvinte uitate," in C. Dobrogeanu-Gherea, *Scrieri social-politice* (Bucharest: Editura Politică, 1968), p. 212.

[11] C. Dobrogeanu-Gherea, "Socialismul în Romania," in *ibid.*, p. 68.

INTRODUCTION

ever, its use by students of Romanian development in the late nineteenth and early twentieth centuries and by contemporary students of Third World countries points to important weaknesses of this approach. Those who employ an international political economy perspective often underestimate the weight of national or domestic factors in shaping institutional and developmental outcomes. In particular, political economists do not adequately attend to the social and cultural components of dependency. This has resulted in an unnecessarily narrow and misleading conception of dependency.

These "alternative" modes of analysis—i.e., those that tend to emphasize international political economy and those that tend to emphasize sociocultural factors—are significant at the political as well as the theoretical level. An international political economy approach can often serve as an excuse for relative passivity by political reformers who emphasize that they enjoy only a small area of discretion in a context of scarcity and multinational/superpower control. On the other hand, revolutionary aspirants in underdeveloped countries may "find" in the development of international forces bases for social transformation that are absent domestically. Sociocultural analyses may lead to different political stances as well. On the one hand, they may lead to nativist-escapist movements; on the other, to an empirical appreciation of the need to internally reorder major social and cultural features in any serious effort to break through the dependency syndrome. At a more complex level the way in which ideological-political elites combine sociocultural and international political economy perspectives may be used to differentiate them in terms of their relative and distinctive competences (or incompetences) in overcoming the syndrome of dependency. Similarly, the way in which analysts combine these two perspectives may be used to compare their relative insights into the character and dynamics of the dependency phenomenon.

II

STATUS SOCIETIES

One of the most persistent features in the analysis of non-Western countries has been the uncritical use of categories appropriate to Western social reality.[1] It has been the Western intellectuals' version of prismatism. Today there is an equally inappropriate and costly tendency—namely, the denial of a need for ideal-typical distinctions between traditional and modern forms of social orientation and organization. A distinction of this order—one that provides benchmarks for empirical research of what is distinctive in particular developmental experiences—underpins our analysis of dependency. The distinction is that offered by Weber between status and class. The conceptual point of departure in this chapter will be that the major institutions of a peasant country have a status, not class, character. A careful explication of what is and what is not implied by the distinction between status and class is necessary not only because this distinction informs our entire analysis of dependency, but also because distinctions of this type are currently viewed in academia as ethnocentric, ahistorical, ideologically biased, *and* empirically misleading.

According to Weber, "In contrast to the purely economically determined 'class situation' we wish to designate as status situation every typical component of the life of men that is determined by a specific, positive or negative social estimation of honor." In content, "Status honor is normally expressed by the fact that above all else a specific style of life is expected from all those who wish to belong to the circle [and] . . . *specific status honor . . . always rests upon dis-*

---

[1]My colleague Andrew Janos makes the same point in an article on Hungary, "The Decline of Oligarchy: Bureaucratic and Mass Politics in the Age of Dualism (1867-1918)," in *Revolution in Perspective: Essays on the Hungarian Soviet Republic*, eds. Andrew C. Janos and William B. Slottman (Berkeley: University of California Press, 1971), pp. 1-61.

tance and exclusiveness." Classes, unlike status groups, "are not communities; they merely represent the possible and frequent bases for social action. . . . The factor that creates class is unambiguously economic interest and indeed only those interests involved in the existence of the market." Finally, in Weber's formulation status and class are antithetical principles of social organization and action:

> The market and its processes know no personal distinctions. . . . [The market] knows nothing of honor. *The status order means precisely the reverse.* . . . [It] *would be threatened at its very root if mere economic acquisition and naked economic power still bearing the stigma of its extra status origin could bestow upon anyone who has won them the same or even greater honor as the vested interests claim for themselves.*[2]

One can sharpen and develop this Weberian contrast on the basis of other sections of his work and works by other scholars ranging from Coulanges to Polanyi, as well as more recent studies on peasant societies.

From such a review one can outline a general type of traditional or status society that has the following characteristics: (a) The basic unit of social identification and organization is the *corporate group*, which is exclusive in its membership. As Mauss has observed, groups of this order engage in exchanges of various sorts with each other *but* remain distant from and suspicious of each other—i.e., strangers.[3] (b) Relations among such groups are governed by personal—not impersonal—norms of action. Thus integration among groups tends to be based on patrimonial principles,[4] and social ties rest on the personal exchange of gifts, the giving of which can be a means of magical or quasi-magical control[5] and penetration. (c) Consistent

---

[2]See Max Weber, *Economy and Society* (New York: Bedminster Press, 1968), Vol. 2, pp. 926-38. All emphases throughout this book are mine.

[3]Marcel Mauss, *The Gift* (New York: W. W. Norton, 1967), p. 37.

[4]For an example in Latin America, see Richard Morse, "The Heritage of Latin America," in *The Founding of New Societies*, ed. Louis Hartz (New York: Harcourt, Brace & World, 1964), pp. 123-78.

[5]In certain societies gifts may be viewed by the recipient as an integral part of the donor rather than as symbolic objects with no intrinsic or "personal" quality. Consequently, the acceptance of a gift may give the donor a "hold" on the recipient. In this sense exchanges of gifts may be seen by the actors as a magical means of establishing control rather than as a symbolic basis for trust. It is, of course, an empirical matter as to when the exchange of gifts is viewed as a quasi-magical means of control, a culturally prescribed mode of creating trust, or a private convention signifying friendship. The point is that we must be

with and reinforcing this mode of social organization and integration, the division of labor tends to be characterized by a categoric or stereotypical assignment of tasks (i.e., by caste, ethnic, occupational, or other ascriptive quality). (d) With this type of social organization and division of labor, a status society tends to have an ontology that stresses the concrete and discrete—i.e., discontinuous—quality of social reality. Both social organization and social thought vary for the most part within the boundaries set by generalization. Sociopolitical integration on the basis of second-order abstract principles is as exceptional as intellectual statements that go beyond generalization to abstraction and synthesis. (e) In a world seen to be comprised of concrete and discrete elements—that is, indivisible units—economic, social, cultural, and political resources are seen as being finite and immobile rather than expanding and flexible. This orientation—which has at its core a zero-sum appreciation of transactions in all spheres[6]—has at its base not simply the resource-poor character of peasant societies, but also the corresponding religious-magical notions that the world is comprised of units (natural, social, material) each of which has its appropriate, indivisible essence.

It goes without saying that a society of this order nowhere exists (or has existed) in pure form. The definition of religious and/or magical conceptions, the domains in which they were influential, and the degree and regularity of resource scarcity—all vary in place and time. However, it is equally important that with the exception of Western Europe—in particular Western Europe since the nineteenth century[7]—the greater part of the world has varied in its social

careful to examine—not simply assume—the meaning(s) parties to an exchange bring to that act.

[6]George Foster has termed this orientation the "image of limited good." See his seminal article, "Peasant Society and the Image of Limited Good," *American Anthropologist* 65 (April 1965), pp. 293-315.

[7]There is no one time when Western Europe's exceptional institutional and cultural qualities can be said to have originated. Catholicism, feudalism, the development of a particular type of city and citizenship, church-state patterns, the Renaissance, the Reformation, the English and French Revolutions, and the absence of an effective areawide empire from the fifth century on—all can be used to argue the exceptional quality of West European development at particular historical points. I consider the emergence of a market society in the broad sense (i.e., not simply the economic) the "most" important of these developments, in part because it established Western Europe as an authoritative frame of reference with global (not just regional) and sociocultural (not just political-economic) significance.

organization and self-identification *within the terms that make up this ideal-typical syndrome.* Rustow's assertion that "modernity, though a broad concept, can be positively defined ... [not] so its opposite tradition,"[8] is erroneous. Far from being a residual concept, tradition has a generalized empirical basis and theoretical utility. In support of this latter claim, we shall continue to elaborate on the analytic distinction *and* empirical relation between class and status modes of organization.

Weber has outlined some idea of the Western liberal—or market—type of class society. It is a society in which property is very important but not decisive. What *is* decisive is the place and character *of the market as a general social institution.* Weber's point about the market basis of class formation finds its strongest expression in Polanyi's analysis of West European society. Polyani made the crucial observation that

> normally the economic order is merely a function of the social, in which it is contained. Neither under tribal, nor feudal, nor mercantile conditions was there ... a separate economic system in society. *Nineteenth century (Western) society, in which economic activity was isolated and imputed to a distinctive economic motive, was, indeed, a singular departure.*[9]

As Polanyi goes on to note, it was singular not only in imputing to economic activity a distinctive economic motive, but also in subjecting the rest of society to the ethos and principles of economic reasoning.[10]

Abstracting from Weber's and Polanyi's descriptions of the market type of class society, we can point, first, to the development of a society in which the framework of social action is based on *impersonal* norms. In the West this took the institutional form of market and electoral politics. Weber's and Polanyi's analyses of this type of class society suggest a second, equally important development. In a market-class society *a fundamental change in the framework of social action is complemented by a change in the basic units of social identification, organization, and action.* In a class society the basic units of social identification, organization, and action are the in-

[8]Dankwart A. Rustow, *A World of Nations* (Washington, D. C.: The Brookings Institution, 1967), pp. 11-12.

[9]Karl Polanyi, *The Great Transformation* (Boston: Beacon Press, 1965), p. 71.

[10]*Ibid.* See in particular the contrast between market and mercantilist society (pp. 70-71).

dividual and the nuclear family, not the corporate group (familial or otherwise).

In a truly exceptional piece of research and analysis, James Obelkevich has recently examined the transformations that occurred between 1825 and 1875 in a rural area of England (South Lindsey). He focuses on the relations between religion and social organization in an era of commercialization and economic development. While Obelkevich is highly sensitive to the uneven, amalgam-like quality of social change in the region, he repeatedly emphasizes the move from a village society in which "the community or collectivity was in important ways prior to the individuals who composed it"[11] to one in which classes were made "not only by acting on common economic interests *but also by withdrawing from the village community . . . and by retreating into the private life of the family and of individual experience.*"[12] This change did not occur among all strata at the same rate, or with the same degree of thoroughness, or with identical meanings attached, but it fundamentally altered the character of local life. This alteration had a distinguishing feature. In Obelkevich's words: "If one theme is to be selected, it is the decline of the 'crowd' and the complex rise of individualism."[13]

I would suggest that the emergence of the individual and the nuclear family as the basic unit of social action, identification, and organization is a primary criterion of what we have termed class society. What Deutsch terms social mobilization[14] —the uprooting of people and their availability for recommitment to new identities— refers in general to the creation of more extensive identities, and in the West to the uprooting of social-corporate forms of organization based on status and the development of organizations based on the role-playing individual. (*However*, while the appearance of the individual-nuclear family as the basic unit of social action and identification is a primary criterion of a class or modern society, the *type* of individualism will vary with the *particular institutional definition* impersonal norms are given in each society.)

Just as in a status society the corporate character of the basic

---

[11]James Obelkevich, *Religion and Rural Society: South Lindsey 1825-1875* (Oxford: Clarendon Press, 1976), p. 24.

[12]*Ibid.*, p. 25.

[13]*Ibid.*, p. 92.

[14]Karl Deutsch, "Social Mobilization and Political Development," *American Political Science Review* LV, 3 (September 1961): 493-514.

STATUS SOCIETIES

units of social identification and action shapes the other (i. e., political, economic, intellectual) features of society, so in a class society the central role of the individual and nuclear family shapes the mode of organization and adaptation. Yet however clear the analytic distinctions between these two types of societies may be, empirically one finds in societies that approximate one type features that are supposedly mutually exclusive. For example, in what would be considered a status or honor-oriented society, wealth is not simply an incidental factor but rather an integral part of the self-conception and operation of that society. As a case in point, in *The Iliad* the heroic warrior elites of a status-based society are continually attending to considerations of wealth, and they have to be regularly reminded that plunder comes only after battle.[15] In any case, whether before or after battle, it is quite clear that plunder is an integral part of the heroic exercise. Nor is there much doubt about the economic standing and concerns of the major combatants: "Amphios, Selagos' son, who rich in possessions and rich in cornland" fought on the Trojan side, was far from an atypical figure.[16] From ancient Troy to contemporary Senegal is quite a leap. Yet the behavior of contemporary Sufi saints or Mouride Brothers in Senegal presents another striking instance of a charismatic group for whom wealth is an integral element of status. According to O'Brien, "Saintly charisma or *baraka* . . . is seen by the disciples above all in material terms."[17] The examples could be extended, but the point is clear: in most status-based societies the accumulation of wealth is an integral and defining element of social organization and behavior. What is by no means clear is the *meaning* of that behavior and the *role* assigned to wealth in status societies.

The emphasis on the gaining and display of wealth has not escaped those who argue for a fundamental difference between status and class societies. In *The Protestant Ethic* Weber pointed out that "the greed of the Chinese Mandarin, the old Roman aristocrat,

---

[15]*The Iliad of Homer*, trans. Richard Lattimore (Chicago: University of Chicago Press, 1957), p. 155.

[16]*Ibid.*, p. 144.

[17]Donal B. Cruise O'Brien, *Saints and Politicians* (New York: Cambridge University Press, 1975), p. 77. Of course one must be sensitive to differences in perceptions between disciples and masters. However, as O'Brien notes, the masters signal their charismatic status in part through the display afforded by wealth.

or the modern peasant can stand up to any comparison."[18] Weber's Dutch sea-captain, who "would go through hell for gain, even though he scorched his sails," has had counterparts in all areas of the world from *The Iliad* on. Weber pointed out not only that "capitalistic acquisition as an adventure has been at home in all types of economic society which have known trade with the use of money," *but also that "absolute and conscious ruthlessness in acquisition has often stood in the closest connection with the strictest conformity to tradition."*[19] It is the latter point that warrants close attention. Status-based societies do not lack groups oriented toward acquisition, capable of calculation, and possessing economic intelligence. In the middle of *The Iliad*, in the midst of heroic battles (with gods roaming about and with issues of honor always at stake), one comes across two warriors intent upon establishing a personal bond. They do so by exchanging armor—an intimate and meaningful act. This does not prevent the author from noting that "Zeus . . . stole away the wits of Glaukos who exchanged with Diomedes . . . armor of gold for bronze, for nine oxen's worth, the worth of a hundred."[20]

Thus it is not the presence or absence of economic calculation that matters most in distinguishing the social organization of status from class societies. What is most critical is that in the context of status-based societies the mode of acquisition of wealth, its use, and the perception of its character differ radically and decisively from the same features in class-based societies. Wealth is significant in status societies as conspicuous display, as a demonstration of power in a world of scarcity (thus the significance of a politics of largesse from ancient Athens to "big man" politics in contemporary Africa),[21] and as a proof of the magical-religious powers of the person or group possessing it.[22] (On the last point, in societies

---

[18]Max Weber, *The Protestant Ethic and the Spirit of Capitalism* (New York: Charles Scribner's Sons, 1958), p. 56.

[19]*Ibid.*, p. 58

[20]*The Iliad of Homer*, p. 159.

[21]On ancient Greece see W. Robert Connor's excellent book *The New Politicians of Fifth-Century Athens* (Princeton, N. J.: Princeton University Press, 1971), pp. 18-22. On Africa see Robert Price's valuable study, "Politics and Culture in Contemporary Ghana: The Big Man-Small Boy Syndrome," *Journal of African Studies* 1, 2 (Summer 1974): esp. 173-84.

[22]See Mauss, *passim*.

where reality is seen in concrete and discrete terms, and where generalization not abstraction is the typical mode of intellectual speculation, material objects are often seen as possessing characters of their own. Analysts of such societies must be sensitive to this possibility and realize that in these settings wealth may have to be interpreted in terms of an economic theology.)[23]

In status-based societies there is calculation for gain, but not the calculation of individuals based on impersonal, procedural norms. Economic behavior is informed by an heroic-plunder-largesse mentality. This behavior takes a variety of forms, but it differs in kind from the impersonal-procedural mode of continuous and exact transactions that characterizes modern or class societies. Thus when one comes across a statement by Bates in his *Rural Responses to Industrialization* (in Zambia) that "much of the behavior of rural dwellers is based upon their desire for material gain," there is no reason to share the author's impression that something highly novel has been discovered. Bates (and his case is fairly typical today) says that in making his assertion, he departs "from the tradition that interprets the behavior of rural dwellers as being largely determined by cultural beliefs, the forces of tradition or religious values." Furthermore, he rejects "the interpretation of rural behavior that views villagers as too lazy, irrational, or unmotivated to take advantage of expanding economic opportunities."[24] I reject it also, but it should be clear that the distinction between tradition and modernity—or status and class—does not rest on such contrasts. The notion of status society that we are working with does not obscure the role of acquisition, calculation, or wealth, any more than it obscures the incidence of tension and conflict within and among the groups that make up a village, clan, or status-based state. But it can prevent an observer from confusing the universal importance of economic behavior with a conclusion that all societies are basically alike. *The meaning of behavior is established through reference to a society's framework of social action and basic units of social identification and organization. Where that framework is based on impersonal norms of social action and the individual is the basic unit of identification and organization, a class society exists. Where that framework is based on personal norms of social action and the corporate group is the basic unit of identification and organization, a status society exists.*

[23]*Ibid.*, pp. 41-43.

[24]Robert H. Bates, *Rural Responses to Industrialization: A Study of Village Zambia* (New Haven: Yale University Press, 1976), p. 2.

THE LENINIST RESPONSE TO NATIONAL DEPENDENCY

Empirically one can find instances of behavior that *appear* to be identical in status and class societies (e.g., calculated accumulation of wealth). However, one must be aware of the danger of confusing form with substance, and in the absence of ideal-typical distinctions, one is unlikely to note the confusion. The value of an ideal-typical statement about the place and meaning of wealth in a status-based society is that (a) it provides benchmarks by which to ascertain the character of a given institutional/cultural configuration, and (b) it provides the analyst with an appreciation of the central meanings in a social pattern that make formally similar phenomena (e.g., calculating behavior to accumulate wealth) substantively distinct. In a passage on the importance and particular quality of political friendship in fifth-century Greece, Connor makes precisely this point:

> It is not that considerations of economic interest, class loyalty, or patriotic concern did not operate [in Athenian politics]. . . . It would be a strange world indeed where these were entirely eliminated. They were surely present in Athens, *but in a way that differs significantly from what we moderns expect.* These considerations found expression through friendship groups . . . and the groups gave voice to the economic and social concerns of their members. Modern analogies are easy to find, but they deceive us in some important respects.[25]

All of this is *not* to say there are not any societies in which status and class types of calculation and accumulation *coexist.* However, if our definition of the differences between the organization and orientation of status and class societies has merit, then we would expect relations between groups oriented and organized along status and class lines to be potentially or actually in conflict. (For example, it is not formally possible for a social institution such as the family to be simultaneously nuclear and corporate.) This is not to assert that empirically one will not find institutional amalgams of orientations that in ideal-typical terms are antithetical. *However, it is to assert that such amalgams are conflict-relations*—what might be termed *kto-kovo* encounters.[26] Organizations and practices of a status and class nature can institutionally coexist *but only under coercive auspices,* of which three forms can be readily identified:

---

[25] Connor, p. 31. Connor's point is that neither the pursuit of economic gain nor the quality of political friendship is the same as in industrial-liberal societies.

[26] *Kto-kovo* signifies conflict between antithetical forces in which the outcome favored by each is domination.

compartmentalization, domination, and displacement. In the first instance—compartmentalization—modern enclaves that do not directly threaten the material or ideal interests of elites and institutions in a status-based society can coexist with them. In the second instance—domination—where the weight of one type of organization and practice is clearly superior, the weaker but threatening type *will be coopted and used to extend the power and scope of the stronger type*.[27] In the third instance—displacement—where a society is based on groups with different principles of organization, relatively equal in strength, and interacting on a continuous basis, one can expect an externalization of the conflict through imperialism, internal displacement through fascism, or civil war.

Enough has been said at this point about the formal dimensions of status and class as principles of social identification and organization and about the formal aspects of their interaction. What is needed now is an empirical referent that will enable us to develop and critically evaluate these terms and modes of analysis in relation to the phenomenon of dependency. Many of the observations made in the preceding section can be developed in the context of both the Romanian experience and the experience of non-European, ex-colonial peasant countries.

In his analysis of Romanian village organization, Mihail Cernea emphasizes the key role of the corporate peasant family household. His analysis stresses several familiar points: (a) the peasant corporate household provided the fundamental principle and mode of socio-economic and cultural organization during the interwar period; (b) with the intrusion of market elements, the institutional form of village life changed, but the family remained the basic work unit, and commercial relations were undertaken in the context of familial principles of organization and orientation; (c) the major consequence of the dominance of the peasant corporate household economically and the familial model socially and culturally was *the unintelligibil-*

---

[27]Note that there is no assumption that *class* orientations, organizations, and groups will inexorably dominate traditional or *status* orientations, organizations, and groups. The only assumption is that the interaction is always conflictual. The expectation is that the conflict's intensity will reflect how important the elements in contact are to the respective paradigms. The more central the elements, the more intense the conflict.

THE LENINIST RESPONSE TO NATIONAL DEPENDENCY

ity for and resistance of the peasants to operating in a framework of impersonal rules.[28]

The features of peasant society that Cernea emphasizes were addressed earlier by the economist Virgil Madgearu and others (though not always in as clear an analytic style or with as much systematic empirical evidence). The picture drawn is of a society vertically integrated along village and familial lines rather than horizontally along class lines—a kind of integration that Shanin in his excellent study of the Russian peasantry argues is characteristic of peasant society.[29]

One finds a society in which *wealth is subordinated to status*, and the conspicuous display of wealth is required as evidence of status. In her study of the Transylvanian village of Izvor, Katherine Verdery examined the basis of status rankings among Romanian (and German) villagers. Several of her findings are relevant here. One of them involves the expression used in the village to indicate prestige. According to Verdery, an *om vazut* (literally, a "visible man") in Izvor "is the archetype of a man with prestige. *Visibility* is a, perhaps *the*, salient attribute of status." Wealthier peasants in Izvor "tended to live in the central part of the village, where social activity was heightened . . . and where 'visibility' was automatic." Verdery goes on to note that "in this system personal conduct accounted for little. . . . Sound character and . . . comportment were often attributed to wealthy households."[30] Significant here is the extent of differentiation by rank or status—not performance—within a social order based on corporate familial units.

The social organization of Romanian society before World War II has parallels in the status of differentiation of traditional Akan

---

[28] Mihail Cernea, *Sociologia cooperativei agricole de producție* [The sociology of collective farms] (Bucharest, 1974); see particularly the chapter on the social organization of the traditional Romanian village ("Organizarea sociala a satului traditional"), pp. 43-58.

[29] Teodor Shanin, *The Awkward Class* (Oxford: The Clarendon Press, 1972). This is a most important contribution to developmental—not simply Russian-Soviet—studies. Like Shanin's book, Gregory Massell's *The Surrogate Proletariat* (Princeton: Princeton University Press, 1974) and Merle Fainsod's *Smolensk Under Soviet Rule* (New York: Vintage Russian Library, 1958) should not be restricted to students of Soviet development.

[30] "Ethnic Stratification in the European Periphery: The Historical Sociology of a Transylvanian Village " (Ph. D. dissertation, Department of Anthropology, Stanford University, December 1976), pp. 250, 253-54.

and contemporary Ghanaian society as observed by Price.[31] In both one finds a "big man-small boy" syndrome, in which those excluded from possessing prestige and wealth defer to the arbitrary behavior of those possessing them.[32] During the interwar period in Romania and the rest of Eastern Europe, this pattern of "big man" and corporate status was institutionalized in the form of a political-bureaucratic ruling class clearly distinguished from the mass of the population by dress, wealth, power, and (often) language.

The presence and power of status organization and orientation were nowhere better demonstrated in Romania than in the type of economic development that occurred in the late nineteenth and early twentieth centuries. In this realm more than in any other the exceptional quality of *West* European development became apparent to most Romanian observers. Almost without exception Romanian intellectuals noted that Romanian economic development occurred under very different auspices than those that characterized nineteenth-century Western Europe. Romania, East Europe, and the rest of the non-Western world "skipped" the nineteenth century in the sense that, unlike Western Europe, no revolutionary reversal of social and economic orders took place. Only in Western Europe—particularly in England—did a "market society"—as opposed to a society with markets—come into existence.[33] Significantly, Ştefan Zeletin, who argued more vociferously than anyone that Romania was following the classical Western pattern of mercantilism, liberalism, and imperialism, noted one critical difference—namely, in the West the bourgeoisie was formed in opposition to the central political power, while in Romania the bourgeoisie confounded itself with the ruling elite in the form of a ruling oligarchy (*"burghezia se desvoltă din chiar sânul acesteia: din oligarchie"*).[34] This is *the* critical difference and explains what Zeletin notes—namely, that Romanian development was characterized by a move directly from mercantilism to finance capitalism. In Zeletin's view Romania "did not pass through

---

[31]Price, pp. 173-204. Romanian and Ghanaian social institutions were not identical; rather, their structural and cultural patterns were similar.

[32]This personal hierarchical relationship is central to pre-industrial societies across cultures and time.

[33]See Polanyi. His efforts to specify the distinctiveness of Western development rank with Weber's.

[34]Ştefan Zeletin, *Burghezia română* (Bucharest: Cultura Naţională, 1925), p. 81.

the intermediary phase of liberalism, of real decentralization and democracy."[35] *Romania, like the rest of the non-Western world, failed to experience the revolution of a market society—in contrast to the disrupting effects of market-commercial forces.* For Romania and Eastern Europe, capitalism meant political-mercantilist capitalism, not the capitalism of the Protestant ethic. In Romania capitalism was institutionally different but structurally similar to the pattern of economic organization described by Weber as political capitalism in his distinction between Puritan capitalism and the mercantile capitalism of the Stuarts.[36]

The continuing debate in Romania over whether or not there was a Romanian bourgeoisie was a debate over the character of social and economic development. Madgearu, a leading member of the Peasant Party, began his *Agrarianism, Capitalism, şi Imperialism* by noting the exceptional quality of England's mode of economic development.[37] Madgearu correctly stated that unlike England, Romania's economic development had never lost its mercantilist quality—by which he meant an emphasis on state control, monopolies, and privileges granted to specific individuals and companies. In the same vein, the Social Democrat Şerban Voinea noted that instead of making financial capital available to industrialists, the Romanian liberal oligarchy introduced "political despotism in the economic domain" by treating the budget and state as its "holding."[38] This comment describes the process of economic development in most non-Western settings. In all these respects capitalism in Romania shared the features of capitalism in contemporary Third World regimes. As Elliot Berg has pointed out, capitalism in colonial Africa was "dirigiste, antifree enterprise to the core,"[39] and in his stimulating study of contemporary Kenya Leys quite convincingly

---

[35]Zeletin, p. 157. Şerban Voinea quickly and correctly pointed out that this "departure" from the Western pattern undermined Zeletin's argument that Romania was faithfully reproducing the Western stages of development (see Ş. Voinea, *Marxism oligarhic* [Bucharest: Editura I. Brănişteanu, 1926], p. 225).

[36]M. Weber, *The Protestant Ethic*, p. 179.

[37]Virgil Madgearu, *Agrarianism, Capitalism, şi Imperialism* (Bucharest: Editura "Economistul," 1936), pp. 9-17.

[38]Voinea, pp. 236-37. In Voinea's words, the oligarchy placed a "desire for gain over the desire for profit."

[39]Elliot J. Berg, "Socialism and Economic Development in Tropical Africa," *Quarterly Journal of Economics* LXXVIII (November 1964): 554.

portrays the encapsulation of commercial capitalism in state and social-tribal frameworks.[40] Polanyi's description of mercantilism as an economic system submerged in general social relations in which market relations are "an accessory feature of an institutional setting controlled and regulated" by social authority is in large part applicable to the situation in Romania and elsewhere in the developing world.[41] In Romania the impact of international commerce and industry significantly altered the *institutional definition* of a rural agrarian society but not the *structural features* of what we have termed a status-based society.

Earlier I suggested that societies organized along status lines have a stereotyped or categoric division of labor in which different ethnic, occupational, and religious strata play rigidly assigned roles and are considered to be unavailable for—and are inappropriately included in—certain types of social action. No clearer example of this can be found than in a statement addressed to a workers' delegation by the Hungarian Minister of the Interior in 1875: "Are you industrial workers? Then you should work industriously. You do not have to bother with anything else. You do not need associations, and if you mix in politics, I will teach you a lesson that you [will] never forget."[42] In Romania (as well as the rest of Eastern Europe) the categoric division of labor was supplemented by a gap in culture that (as already noted) was not only wide, but also of an order quite different from that separating upper and lower classes in Western Europe. In Eugen Weber's words:

> [In Western Europe] the proletariat . . . participated in the industrial revolution not only by their effort but by their inventions [and] shared the cultural background, skills, and language of their masters, [while in] Romania, as in Algeria or Peru, master

---

[40]Leys, esp. chs. 5 and 6. There is an odd flavor to Leys' very good book, the source of which is the conflict between the author's determination to argue that class is the most useful analytic category in understanding contemporary Kenya and the information he presents in the book that clearly points to the subordination of class to status. For example: "In Kenya in 1970 . . . the rich and powerful people in the cities were not yet seen as a race apart; their own rural origins were mostly recent, and while the link between them and the poorest peasants was becoming artificial and mystified, it was still quite active and personal" (p. 190).

[41]Polanyi, p. 67.

[42]Quoted in Janos, p. 42.

and worker belong figuratively and sometimes literally to different nations.[43]

What then was the basis of political integration in Romania and comparable countries? To the extent that a widely shared framework of national identification and organization exists in such countries (and one did exist in the Romanian case), it is *generalized* from the organization of the corporate, patriarchal, peasant household. The scope of identification is obviously larger than for membership in a family, *but it is not different in kind*. The references of national identification were religious and personal, and for the majority of the population they were likely to be understood in terms of mass ("small boy") deference to privileged "big men"—the King and God.

Finally, in Romania—as in other peasant countries—there was a tendency among the intelligentsia to view social reality as discontinuous rather than interdependent. This tendency has not received the attention it warrants. It was by no means exclusively Romanian. Henry Turner's striking comment on the tendency of the Nazis to accord the products of industry a curious sort of autonomy, viewing them largely in isolation from the social, economic, and political concomitants of the processes that made them possible, points to a feature held in common by highly diverse political movements.[44] In the statements and program of Alexander Stamboliiski, one of the most interesting figures in interwar Eastern Europe, there is a call to almost literally destroy the city, to separate it from the countryside[45]—a call that is repeated by Frantz Fanon in *The Wretched of the Earth*,[46] and perhaps in the program of the Khmer

---

[43]"Romania," in *The European Right*, eds. Hans Rogger and E. Weber (Berkeley: University of California Press, 1966), p. 504. Weber does not claim the absence of a cultural gap between classes in Western Europe (it still exists in certain respects between the working and middle classes), but he emphasizes the different character of that gap in Western and certain non-Western settings. For his analysis of the French case, see E. Weber, *Peasants into Frenchmen* (Stanford: Stanford University Press, 1976).

[44]See Henry Ashby Turner, Jr.'s excellent piece "Fascism and Modernization," *World Politics* XXIV, 4 (July 1972): 557.

[45]On Stamboliiski see Joseph Rothschild, *The Communist Party of Bulgaria* (New York: Columbia University Press, 1959), pp. 85-117; a more recent work is John D. Bell, *Peasants in Power: Alexander Stamboliiski and the Bulgarian Agrarian National Union: 1899-1923* (Princeton: Princeton University Press, 1977).

[46]On Frantz Fanon's position see *The Wretched of the Earth* (New York: Grove Press, 1966). Fanon writes: "The life of the capital, an altogether artificial

Rouge in Cambodia today.[47] In Romania Dobrogeanu-Gherea's criticism of the Anarchist tendency to compartmentalize social life in independent categories (*"anarhiştii desfac viaţa socialǎ în categorii independente . . . fǎrǎ a avea în vedere legǎtura strînsǎ ce e între categoriile sociale"*)[48] was applicable to a wide range of national actors, movements, and analysts who attempted to explain and resolve Romania's social, economic, and political problems.

Romania's basic social units, organizational models, and cultural matrices were the peasant household and village community. These were corporate units of identity and membership; "indivisible," clearly bounded units in competition over finite resources and based on personal-affective ties subordinating economic considerations and manipulating them in light of their own status-based meanings; and the social bases for an epistemology that stressed empirical discontinuities in place of interdependence, and an ontology that emphasized the discrete and concrete (vs. abstract) organizations of social reality. The implications of this structure for the character of Romanian state and national development can be best elaborated by directly examining the phenomenon of national dependency in a peasant society.

---

life which is stuck onto the real, national life like a foreign body, ought to take up the least space possible in the life of the nation" (p. 150). One is reminded of the Romanian Iron Guard's notion that the Romanian state was an "invention state."

[47]The decimation of Phnom Penh has a "Fanonian" ideological tinge to it. In addition, it probably reflects the small number of adequately trained cadres available to the Pol Pot regime and able to control a major urban center.

[48]C. Dobrogeanu-Gherea, "Anarhia Cugetarii," in C. Dobrogeanu-Gherea, *Scrieri social-politice*, p. 149.

III

NATIONAL DEPENDENCY IN A PEASANT SOCIETY

It is no exaggeration to say—as Henry Roberts did in his analysis of interwar Romania—that "ever since their emergence as an independent nation the Rumanians have been preoccupied, almost obsessed with the nature of their relation to the west."[1] This preoccupation "took flesh" in the Romanian elite's "cultural infatuation with France and fetishistic fascination with foreign affairs and foreign politico-legal models."[2] In the latter part of the nineteenth century the power and wealth of the West unfolded in a striking and overwhelming fashion. To argue—as Stavrianos has—that "the whole world, in varying proportions, feared, respected, admired, and imitated Europe"[3] is to report a fact that holds in large measure up to the present. John Saul's comment that African elites "ineluctably [face] the West not as masters of their own fate but as apprentices in search of models" is supported by both Ekeh's study of the Nigerian elite and Price's analysis of the Ghanaian military.[4] The most striking feature in all these cases is the marked emulative orientation of a formally sovereign national elite. What are the bases of this often fetish-like emulation?

---

[1] Henry Roberts, *Rumania: Political Problems of an Agrarian State* (New Haven: Yale University Press, 1951), p. 339.

[2] Rothschild, *East Central Europe Between the Two World Wars*, p. 321.

[3] L. S. Stavrianos, "The Influence of the West on the Balkans," in *The Balkans in Transition*, eds. Charles and Barbara Jelavich (Berkeley: University of California Press, 1963), p. 197.

[4] John Saul, "African Socialism in One Country: Tanzania," in *Essays on the Political Economy of Africa*, eds. Giovanni Arrighi and John S. Saul (New York: Monthly Review Press, 1973), p. 290; Peter Ekeh, "Colonialism and the Two Publics in Africa: A Theoretical Statement," *Comparative Studies in Society and History* 17 (January 1975): 91-112; Robert Price, "A Theoretical Approach to Military Rule in New States: Reference Group Theory and the Ghanaian Case," *World Politics* XXIII (April 1971): 339-430.

NATIONAL DEPENDENCY IN A PEASANT SOCIETY

At many points in history certain forms of political organization can be identified that authoritatively establish the political and ideological idiom of an age. Rome, seventeenth-century France, nineteenth-century Britain, twentieth-century America, China at certain points in its history, and the Soviet Union and Fascist Italy for a period of time in the twentieth century—all have been authoritative references, political units whose institutions and ideologies to varying extents have shaped the self-conceptions of what might be termed "retinue elites."[5]

Dependency is a consequence of the premature but imperative adoption of a political format for which the appropriate social base is lacking. The adoption of such a format (e.g., liberal political institutions) is imperative if the adopting country is to be seen, understood, and taken seriously in the international arena. In an era when isolation is no longer possible (Paraguay may be the remaining exception due to its "march" or buffer role), weak countries must adopt formats that allow them to be recognized politically. In order to establish their claims for political survival, economic aid, *and* prestige, weak countries must first be intelligible in an institutional sense to powerful countries in a position to recognize or ignore them. For these reasons, *adoption of the organizational and ideological idiom of the dominant powers becomes situationally necessary.*

In a typical dependent situation the elites of a peasant society—a society based on status organization and orientation—have to secure the recognition of a powerful state, a national "big man." Just as in societies characterized by invidious status inequalities "small boys" must gain the attention of "big men" or patrons in order to survive, *so a small country's adoption of a particular ideological and institutional facade may be as much an effort to make a special claim on a great power in order to survive as a political unit as a choice to redefine its internal sociopolitical organization.*[6] In a brilliant and

---

[5]Political models may exist on a regional as well as international scale. The current role and standing of Saudi Arabia in an area extending from Pakistan to the Sudan is a striking instance of a regional power exercising economic power, religious authority, and political influence on the basis of its economic and religious resources.

[6]My emphasis on the situational necessity of adopting certain institutional facades for purposes of intelligibility in the international arena does not preclude an appreciation of other reasons for the "premature adoption of political formats for which the appropriate social base is lacking." I discuss some of these

23

neglected commentary on Romania's relation to the West, Dobrogeanu-Gherea noted that Romania's adoption of a liberal facade was necessary for Romania to gain the support of West European powers against the danger posed by Russia to Romania's national existence.[7] By adopting liberal institutions and idiom and presenting itself as a parliamentary-commercial nation—in short, *by making itself intelligible and recognizable to the West*—Romania could hopefully find patrons that could check the aspirations of the three empires surrounding it.

Ion C. Brătianu's success after Cuza's fall in 1866 in "engineering the selection of Prince Charles of Hohenzollern as [Cuza's] successor" was in keeping with Romania's attempt to make itself intelligible to the West. Charles was linked to the ruling Prussian dynasty and was a cousin of Napoleon III. As Fritz Stern suggests, this was part of a Romanian effort to "claim for themselves a Western identity."[8] Cuza's self-reliance scheme—dependent on the good will of Austria, Russia, and the Porte[9]—was replaced by an effort to ensure a greater degree of domestic autonomy through a more explicit link with great powers further removed from Romania's borders.

The hypothesis can be advanced that weak countries neighboring powerful and potentially expanding countries, in an effort to nationally differentiate themselves and gain support from non-neighboring great powers, will adopt the ideological and institutional facade of such powers. For example, Benin's adoption of a Marxist-Leninist facade may have more than a little to do with the fact that it borders on "capitalist" and powerful Nigeria.

Efforts by the elites of a peasant status society to secure a relationship with a powerful patron state reflect more than the imperatives of political recognition and intelligibility, however. Efforts

reasons below and others in a forthcoming article on African "Scientific Socialist" regimes. The latter include the association made by certain elites between particular institutional facades and the elites' presumed ability to effectively centralize a fragmented polity and society, the appropriation of new ideological idioms by unestablished elites with little access to the traditional sources of authority, and the tendency of some elites facing desperate economic and social circumstances to fall back on a quasi-magical type of political behavior.

[7]Dobrogeanu-Gherea, *Neoiobagia*, pp. 39-40.

[8]Fritz Stern, *Gold and Iron: Bismarck, Bleichröder, and the Building of the German Empire* (New York: Alfred A. Knopf, 1977), p. 353.

[9]See Lawrence R. Beaber, "Austria and the Emergence of Rumania, 1855-1861," *East European Quarterly* XI (Spring 1977): 65-78.

of this order may also reflect the conceptions of political organization and authority with which elites in many peasant countries work *and* the coincidence between these conceptions and the organization of international life *at particular historical points.*

A striking instance of autonomy considered in client-patron terms is offered by Lattimore in his study of Outer Mongolia. Lattimore suggests that Outer Mongolia's client relationship with the Soviet Union was not just the result of the Soviet Union being more powerful, ideologically omnivorous, or the only power the Mongols could rely on to check Chinese political and cultural hegemony; he adds the interesting observation that

> the outlook not only of nobles and high lamas but of the common people and the leaders who were beginning to emerge among them was still confined within the framework of a feudal society, and the feudal society was still so much the only known form of society *that even "independence" could only be thought of in feudal terms.*[10]

According to Lattimore, Mongol leaders were in the "habit of thinking in dual terms of authority"—i.e., over those below and under those above. This explanation of Mongolian dependency does not preclude an appreciation of other considerations—such as the absence for Mongolia of alternative sources of support, the desire of the Soviet Union to establish hegemony, or the desire of the Mongol leadership to find in the Soviet regime resources for social change that were not available in Outer Mongolia.

One can partially account for the behavior of Cuba's first president, Palma, in terms similar to those used to explain Sukhe Bator's behavior in Outer Mongolia. Palma was accused of *entreguismo* (national selling-out) because of his reliance on U. S. power. Palma responded to the accusations as follows: "For our beloved Cuba it is a hundred times more preferable to have a political dependence that

---

[10] Owen Lattimore, *Nationalism and Revolution in Mongolia* (New York: Oxford University Press, 1955), p. 35. Lattimore continues: "[The Mongol revolutionaries] were at a loss how to move from mere rebellion to revolution involving great economic changes and a sweeping redistribution of power socially until they, too, were able to move with assurance—*and moral assurance was as important as assurance in the form of arms and other aid*—of being backed by a patron of their own. This patron was the new revolutionary order in Russia" (*ibid.*, p. 37).

assures us of the ... gifts of liberty than an independent ... Republic ... discredited ... by periodic civil wars."[11]

Dependency rests on (a) the imperative need to recognize the claims, and formally adjust to the institutional features, of a great power; (b) the desire to utilize the superior resources of that power to accomplish ends that one's domestic social organization precludes; (c) a domestic sociocultural orientation that favors the adoption of an international "big man" patron who is expected to allow national "small boys" to exercise control in their own bailiwicks in return for diffuse services to the patrons;[12] *and* (d) an international arena whose political organization formally coincides with the status organization of a peasant country and consequently reinforces the status conceptions of authority and power held by the local elites. Of course the weighting of these four bases will vary from case to case and over time, and the determination of their role in the emergence of a specific dependency relationship is an empirical, not definitional, task.

Certainly the period of Rumania's emergence as an ethnic-national and state entity *favored a perception of international life in "status" terms*. For the Romanian elite the perception of the international control exercised by the Great Powers at the Congress of Berlin in 1878 was a defining experience. Here the European national "big men" came together to decide (among other things) Romania's fate. With considerable justification Romanian elites could view this as a quite arbitrary—but not unintelligible—exercise of power.

The organization of international life and the behavior of Great Powers corresponded very closely to the domestic features of Romanian social organization and behavior. The international arena was

---

[11]Quoted in Edward Gonzalez, *Cuba Under Castro: The Limits of Charisma* (Boston: Houghton-Mifflin Company, 1974), pp. 27-28.

[12]The dual quality of an international patron-client relationship is usually slighted. Too often the relationship is seen simply in terms of the client's dependence. However, the client typically expects to be allowed the same scope for arbitrary mastery within his own domain that the patron claims in his wider sphere of control. Thus Nkrumah could quite consistently seek the British Queen's approval of his regime in Ghana in the early 1960's, and could resent any moves to interfere in those areas of Ghanaian political life he saw as his domain. Similarly, Houphouet-Boigny's attempts in the Ivory Coast to share in France's prestige and to recognize its power by naming one of Abidjan's two bridges Pont de Charles De Gaulle in no way implied that Houphouet was himself willing to be anything less than a De Gaulle in the Ivory Coast.

not one of individual nations operating in a context of impersonal procedures and egalitarian institutions, or engaged primarily in peaceful, rational economic exchanges; rather it was one of powerful and competing nations calculating how best to increase their prestige and power—at the expense of others—by expanding their economic and military resources, each attempting to minimize the restraints on its own actions and forming alliances based on advantage, necessity, and suspicion.

A status model of "big men" national patrons and "small boy" national clients might add to our understanding of the international relations between the Great Powers and the Balkans in the late nineteenth and early twentieth centuries, as well as our understanding of contemporary relations between Western powers and certain Third World regimes. A model or explanation that considers only diplomatic, military, and/or economic factors can be seriously incomplete. One must also consider behavioral styles and the meanings attached to them by the various participants.[13]

In an international setting with a status-like character and countries such as Romania (with a peasant social organization and ethos), one can adduce several other features of the dependent behavior of (peasant) client-states—for example, a client state's understanding of foreign loans and its adoption of protectionist policies. To reiterate: the sociocultural explanation is by no means exclusive, but it is important and necessary if one is to grasp the possible *meaning* given by elites in a peasant society to what is termed dependent behavior.

For a national elite from a peasant-status milieu, loans from a "big man" state patron may not be viewed as rational economic transactions subject to norms of exact calculation, scheduled repay-

---

[13]If our argument on patron-client relationships is correct, it helps explain the difficulty the United States may be having with Third World elites. I assume that the British and French as patrons have had an easier time with their clients insofar as both parties to the patron-client relationship viewed it in "status" terms. In short, while the relationship between France and one of its former colonies may be unequal, each side is clear about what is expected from the other. In contrast, the United States tends to understand its relationship with Third World elites in "class" terms, with a corresponding emphasis on the contractual, rule, and impersonal dimensions of interstate relations. I would venture to say this has produced a good deal of confusion, anger, and amusement in the ranks of the U. S.'s Third World clients because the two parties to the patron-client relationship have often acted with radically different understandings of what an interstate alliance or partnership entails.

ment, and impersonal treatment; rather, they may be viewed as largesse from a patron to be repayed in various ways. Demands by the patron for adherence to a scheduled repayment may very likely be interpreted as insults and/or perplexing requests.[14]

The adoption of protectionist policies may likewise be explained in part by considerations that are not fully captured by political-economy arguments. Elites in a peasant society, socialized to varying degrees in terms that stress the concrete and discrete quality of social reality and a "limited good" view of values and goods, may be expected to be highly sensitive to the depletion of natural resources. Such sensitivity may be rooted in more than an empirical evaluation of costs and benefits; it may also be rooted in a sense that their national substance is quite literally being taken away.[15]

Protectionist policies may also in part be explained by the insider-outsider distinction made in peasant societies. And viewed from another side of peasant social organization and cultural orientation, the elite's demand for control over the national economy may be seen not only as a necessary instrument in creating a viable national entity, but also as the necessary accompaniment for recognition as a sovereign elite. Just as domestically a peasant must become the head of a household before being recognized as a man, so peasant elites might see possession of the "land"—i.e., the national economy—as the guarantee of their sovereignty.[16] One should not too quickly dismiss as simply metaphoric the statement made by the Romanian Foreign Minister at the time of the Congress of Berlin in response to

---

[14]My colleague Robert Price suggested one example of a misunderstanding of the terms of a patron-client relationship by its participants: the angry reaction of Zaire's President Mobutu against the United States in June 1975, when he claimed the existence of a CIA plot and asked the U. S. ambassador to leave the country. The upshot was an extraordinary loan to Zaire from the United States. Apparently the American government learned the hard way what it *meant* to be seen in "patron" terms by a Third World "client" who was anxious to maintain patron status in his own bailiwick and humiliated by American insistence that he, a "warrior president," be a "good bookkeeper." I am grateful to Thomas Callaghy for information regarding this conflict.

[15]In this light it would be interesting to examine the intense opposition of the Mexican elite early in the twentieth century to oil concessions.

[16]A striking expression of this in Romania today is the absolute value the Party elite attaches to "Plan Sovereignty"—i.e., having absolute control over the national economy—as against being incorporated as a "national sharecropper" in the Soviet-Comecon "latifundia."

European interference over the status of Jews in Romania—"We are masters in our own house"—or the comment made by Brătianu in the 1920's concerning Western treatment of the Romanian economy—"We want to be treated as an adult and not as a minor."[17] I am not arguing for a sociopsychological interpretation of Romanian or dependency behavior; metaphor is no substitute for analysis. What I am suggesting is that in addition to the objectively poor economic and weak military position of peasant countries and the tendency of powerful countries to create spheres of influence, the internal social organization and ethos of a peasant society in conjunction with an international order dominated by "big men" nations of power and wealth acting arbitrarily in their own interests adds a dimension to our understanding of the dependency phenomenon.

The status character of peasant social organization and cultural orientation does not only contribute to the dependency phenomenon in terms of elite conceptions of political autonomy. *More importantly, it directly affects the types of domestic power elites in a peasant country have available to them in any effort to create an effective institutional base for the formally modern facades they have adopted.*

Dependent societies are by no means stagnant. Zeletin's descriptions of the speed and extent of Romanian development and social change in the nineteenth and early twentieth centuries are exaggerated but not without foundation. Roberts has pointed out that beginning in the mid-nineteenth century the Romanian economy began a dynamic process of change, and Shanin has noted the same situation in Russia.[18]

Nor are dependent societies socially quiescent. In his recent work on Zaire Herbert Weiss has suggested that political science studies of developing nations have tended to ignore the rural radicalism that exists in dependent countries. (Weiss' work focuses on the Kwilu rebellion headed by Pierre Mulélé.)[19] Rothschild's survey of Eastern Europe in the interwar period points to the rural radicalism throughout the area, and his description of Stamboliiski's

---

[17]Quoted in Stern, p. 380, and Roberts, p. 122, respectively.

[18]Shanin, esp. pp. 9-18.

[19]Herbert Weiss, *Political Protest in the Congo* (Princeton: Princeton University Press, 1967), pp. 292-99.

movement in Bulgaria provides a striking illustration of the phenomenon.[20] In Romania, the 1907 peasant uprising, the success of the Iron Guard, Mihalache's peasant party, and (to a lesser extent) the Ploughman's Front—all testify to the existence of a far from passive or inert rural sector.[21]

Nor could one argue that within dependent countries there was inadequate recognition among intellectuals of development problems. Radulescu-Motru's call for a national culture to sustain Romania's formally independent status anticipated Fanon's argument that only the development of a national culture can prevent the development of a dependency situation.[22] Zeletin's argument that Romania could escape "dependence" only if it created a viable national economy anticipated Reginald Green's similar argument about Tanzania.[23] And politically efforts were made to provide a more effective base for Romanian sovereignty.

All of these things notwithstanding, by World War II Romania had not progressed from the stage of imitation to that of originality—to use the Romanian historian Eugen Lovinescu's terms.[24] Rural protests, political initiatives, economic developments, and intellectual appraisals—all occurred under a particular set of sociocultural institutional auspices that shaped and constrained the character and impact of each.

No better illustration of the character and limitations of a peasant country such as Romania can be found than in its state

[20]Rothschild, *East Central Europe Between the Two World Wars*, pp. 334-41, and *The Communist Party of Bulgaria*, pp. 85-117; see also Bell, esp. chs. 1-3.

[21]See Roberts, *passim*.

[22]Radulescu-Motru, p. 140. Radulescu-Motru's statements on political culture, though at times archaic in their phrasing, are in general highly perceptive. Fanon's position on the need for a national culture if independence is to be real can be found in *The Wretched of the Earth*, pp. 165-201.

[23]Zeletin, p. 120; Reginald Herbold Green, "Political Independence and the National Economy: An Essay on the Political Economy of Decolonisation," in *African Perspectives*, eds. Christopher Allen and R. W. Johnson (Cambridge: The University Press, 1970), pp. 273-325. Zeletin argued that with the achievement of political independence in 1877 nothing was more natural than a desire to achieve economic independence—without which political independence was illusory ("*fără care cea politică e numai iluzorie*"). Zeletin concludes: "An agricultural country, even if it enjoys formal independence, is in reality a provincial vassal of the capitalist metropole which provides it with capital and goods" (p. 120). [My translation.]

[24]Lovinescu, pp. 479-80.

organization. The Romanian state's policies and structural relation to Romanian society reflected the status features of the society as a whole. The state functioned as an international diplomatic personage, and in that respect it was the most prominent and powerful corporate "gatekeeper" in a society that rested on a whole series of corporate "gatekeepers." Just as the national elite monopolized access to the Romanian national economy, so a plethora of sub-elites monopolized access to a variety of "closed" social domains within the society. In a compartmentalized society, the state was the largest and most powerful compartment, but a compartment nonetheless. The consequence of this form of social organization was that a relatively limited amount of power was available in the society and to the state. Social, political-bureaucratic, and economic elites were able to successfully immobilize the resources under their control. Dobrogeanu-Gherea's observation that "neo-serfdom" was first and foremost connected with the immobility of the peasant can be given a more general cast. Societies based on status principles of organization are inflexible societies. The predominance of personal vs. impersonal norms of social action greatly limits the range and quality of social interaction, organization, and adaptation.

To say this is not to argue that status or traditional societies are incapable of adaptation. It is to argue that their power to combine diverse social and material resources in novel ways—i. e., their combinatorial freedom—is restricted relative to that of class or modern societies, where the individual is the basic unit of social action and impersonal norms provide the framework of social action. Status-based societies are less able than class-based societies to *standardize* intrinsically diverse social and material resources (in the way the market or due process does in handling highly heterogeneous materials and social units) and interchange and combine them in novel ways. In the absence of an impersonal set of social action and organizational premises, the occasions when the naturally diverse quality of social units (religious, occupational, racial, ethnic) can be mobilized along a common basis in a status society are very limited. The power of a class-based society rests precisely in the existence of frames of reference (i.e., citizen, economic good) that allow for the regular mobilization, standardization, and interchange of diverse units.

The Romanian economy and polity was organized by neither plan nor market. *It was parcelled rather than organized.* The state was an instrument for recognizing or ignoring new claimants on the national patrimony—claimants who (consistent with a corporate-status orientation) requested a protected and privileged place in the neo-mercantilist political economy. In this respect the Romanian political economy was typically extensive in character. Its growth and stability rested on a capacity to provide additional protected spheres of operation for new neo-corporate groups seeking economic, social, and political entry. In comparable fashion, Romanian political life was parcelled into discrete cliques, patron-client chains, and ministerial "fiefs." In short, the major obstacle to Romanian development was the structural principle on which it was socially based: the principle of status, which led to an organization of society on the basis of compartmental corporate and personal units.

In his analysis of Yugoslavia, Rothschild contrasts the Bosnian and Slovenian approaches to political organization and action. The Bosnians "early developed a 'clientele strategy' of supporting whomever was ruling them . . . in return for favors and concessions," while the literate and modern Slovenians had "learned the arts of bargaining and maneuvering coalitions."[25] This contrast has a more general applicability: It can be a contrast between an organization informed by personal norms and one informed by impersonal norms. It could be extended to argue that societies with few economic and population resources organized around and oriented to *personal* norms of social action will be *dependent* societies, while societies with few economic and population resources organized around and oriented to *impersonal* norms of social action will be *weak* societies.

If Romania was to stop being a dependent state, then a new social paradigm was necessary—with its attendant consequences in terms of cultural ethos, units of social action and identity, state organization and its relation to society, and epistemological and ontological orientations. The distinguishing features of this new paradigm would include a mode of social organization that emphasized the individual rather than the social corporate group, saw the world as made up of interdependent (not self-contained) and abstract (not concrete) units, considered goods and values to be expanding (not limited), stressed empirical rather than quasi-magical means of dealing with social reality, and conceived of organization and interaction in impersonal rather than personal terms.

Of critical importance here is the *particular agent under whose*

[25]Rothschild, *East Central Europe Between the Two World Wars*, p. 208.

auspices this new paradigm would be institutionally elaborated. Agents of change are never neutral in character; all significant change entails the mobilization of effort and commitment among some part of a population. Thus the creation of a new social paradigm always occurs under partisan auspices.[26] No better example exists than the highly partisan auspices under which capitalism emerged in Western Europe. The combination of fervent Puritans and mercantilist states provided a far from neutral umbrella for its "inevitable" development. As a new socioeconomic and political paradigm, capitalism was shaped in its institutional and cultural features by its very partisan midwives. However, it is not partisanship *per se* that differentiates radical agents of change from one another. What differentiates them is the manner and extent to which they *combine* elements of intense opposition to the institutional and cultural features of their society with organizational and ideological elements that coincide in certain respects with the structure of the society they wish to transform. Ironically, the very features of most radical right agents of change that make them culturally and politically acceptable at certain times to a status-based society also limit their power to substitute institutions and an ethos based on impersonal norms.[27]

---

[26]That the creation of a new social order should occur under partisan auspices simply emphasizes the fact that for an existing institutional order to be actively opposed, adherents of a new movement must be sustained in their efforts by a belief of great intensity because their efforts will be met with hostility and ostracism.

[27]The Nazis are the exception here. On their revolutionary qualities, see Ralf Dahrendorf, *Society and Democracy in Germany* (New York: Doubleday, 1967), pp. 402-19, and Turner.

IV

THE LENINIST RESPONSE

In both liberal and Leninist regimes (in contrast to peasant-status societies), social action is primarily oriented to impersonal norms.[1] What is particular about Leninist regimes is that impersonality is not expressed in procedural values and rules (i. e., due process), but rather in the *charismatic impersonality of the party organization*. *The novelty of Leninism as an organization is its substitution of charismatic impersonality for the procedural impersonality dominant in the West.*

The concept of charismatic impersonality is not readily digested because it seems to be a contradiction in terms. The reaction to it is likely to be simple rejection, or a redefinition in terms that are more familiar, such as the routinization of charisma. But routinization is not what we are talking about. Our focus (at least at this point) is on the unit designated as having extraordinary powers and "worthy" of loyalty and sacrifice. In Leninism, that unit is THE Party.

As a means of demonstrating that the Leninist party is novel in character, we shall offer a new and operational definition of charisma, contrast Leninism with Nazism, and develop the notion of the "correct line" as a character-defining feature of Leninist organization.

---

[1]This does not mean that liberal and Leninist regimes are the only conceivable means of establishing impersonal norms as authoritative action referents and determinants. However, I am impressed by the *lack of success* most other types of regimes in peasant societies have had in attempting to create a nationally effective set of institutions based on impersonal norms. To argue that Leninist regimes have been successful in this direction is not to argue that all spheres of social life are influenced to the same extent by these norms, that informal behavior based on personalistic norms does not exist, or that the definition and efficacy of such norms is not subject to developmental considerations.

Charisma is not a concept that has suffered benign or any other kind of neglect. Nor should it. Discussion of it continues because it is a central feature of behaviors that recur and are seen as politically and socially significant.

For us there is one striking and defining quality of charismatic leaders. *A charismatic leader dramatically reconciles incompatible commitments and orientations.* It is in this sense that the charismatic is a revolutionary agent—someone who is able in certain social circumstances to *institutionally* combine (with varying degrees of success for varying degrees of time) orientations and commitments that until then were seen as mutually exclusive. It is the extraordinary and inspirational quality of such a leader that makes possible the *recasting of previously incompatible elements into a new unit of personal identity and organizational membership*, and the recommitment of (some) social groups to that unit.

Christ created a new unit—the Church—through his recasting of elements that before had been mutually exclusive—namely, commitment to Judaism as a corporate and parochial ethnic identity and incorporation of the Gentile world. For a significant range of social groups, Christ *recast the terms of personal identity and organizational membership*. To argue this is not to suggest that historical events did not play a critical role in the evolution of this doctrine and organization. Events after Christ's death make the importance of historical contingency quite clear.[2] One does not have to slight history or sociology in order to make the central point: for the comparativist (in contrast to the theologian), Christ's innovation was to combine in an inspirational fashion elements that had previously been mutually exclusive. He created a new unit of membership.

Hitler did with German nationalism and "Aryanism" what Christ did with Jews and Gentiles. The tension between Hitler's commitment to German nationalism and "Aryanism" is a defining quality of his movement. Hitler's orientation was not simply or exclusively to the German nation. Rather, he brought together in ideology and organization (e.g., in the SS) orientations and commitments that had been in critical respects and under different auspices highly conflictual—the exclusivity of ethnic-nationalism and that of "racial, supraethnic exclusivity."

If this conception of the defining quality of a charismatic

---

[2]See, for example, Hugh J. Schonfield, *The Pentecost Revolution* (London: Macdonald and Jane's St. Giles House, 1974), *passim.*

leader is correct, one would predict that upon such a leader's death, his movement would be subject to splits representing the individual conflicting elements the leader had been able to unite. Thus, on Christ's death his movement should have split into a "Jewish" and a "Gentile" faction. It did. The circumstances of Hitler's death make a parallel observation difficult. But even during his lifetime, one could observe some groupings more oriented to German nationalism (e.g., army factions) and others to a transnational "Aryan" line (e.g., SS members).

Lenin took the fundamentally conflicting notions of individual heroism and organizational impersonalism and recast them in the form of an organizational hero—the Bolshevik party. His "party of a new type" was just that: a recasting of orientations that remained conflictual but were no longer mutually exclusive.[3] Lenin's innovation was to create an organization and membership effectively committed to conflicting practices—command and obedience with debate and discussion; belief in inexorable laws of historical change with empirical investigation of social development; heroic action with a persistent concern for the scientific and sober operation of an economy and society; *and an emphasis on individual revolutionary heroism with an emphasis on the superordinate impersonal authority of the Party, itself the central heroic actor and focus of emotional commitment.*

The manner and extent to which these different elements have been institutionally combined have varied significantly in the developmental history of the Soviet and Soviet-type regimes.[4] Yet crucial as the variations are, any attempt to grasp their significance depends on an appreciation of the central element in Lenin's innovation: the conflictual but effective recasting of charismatic-heroic and organizational-impersonal orientations in the form of a party in which heroism is defined in organizational, not individual terms.

To argue that the novelty of Leninism as a political form is that it effectively recasts the mutually exclusive elements of indi-

---

[3] "Democratic Centralism" was for Lenin what "Nazi Germanism" was for Hitler and "Gentile Messiah" for Christ—i.e., *a recasting of mutually exclusive elements into a conflictually based but practically effective new paradigm of membership and action.*

[4] I have outlined a model with static and dynamic features to account for the variations in K. Jowitt, "Inclusion and Mobilization in European Leninist Regimes," *World Politics* XXVIII, 1 (October 1975): esp. 69-71.

vidual heroism and organizational impersonalism is not to say there have not been historical precedents, nor is it to say that such an institutional amalgam of charismatic and modern orientations is constantly weighted in the same fashion. Religious organizations such as the Jesuits and Benedictines and military organizations such as the Marines are in certain respects instances of charismatic impersonalism. And as we have suggested at several points, Leninist regimes weight and define charismatic and modern orientations quite differently over time. What is distinctive about Leninism as an instance of charismatic impersonalism—i. e., as an institutional amalgam of charismatic and modern orientations—is that both these orientations are central to its definition. This contrasts with religious organizations whose secular-empirical orientations are ideally subordinate to non-material, supernatural rationales. This argument obviously does not apply to a military organization, such as the Marines, that combines heroic orientations and technical-secular ones. However, the central place of war as a defining orientation for such an organization differentiates it from a Leninist party. To be sure, the revolutionary commitments of a Leninist party can be seen as comparable—and at certain points identical—to a war-orientation. However, the Party's equally strong commitments to industrialization, scientific development, and economic planning as more than adjuncts to a war mission suggest an organization of a different order.

The difference among these types of charismatic-impersonal organizations then is by no means absolute, but it is significant. As suggested, it lies in the greater consistency that characterizes the place and role of modern elements in the Leninist amalgam. In ideal terms, these elements are less ad hoc, less instrumental, and more central to Leninism as a form of charismatic impersonalism.

To sustain an argument that Lenin's innovation as a charismatic leader was to create a political organization whose defining feature was charismatic impersonalism, one must come to grips with two outstanding and central "challenges" from Soviet history. The most obvious challenge to the argument presented here is Stalin's personal-charismatic role from the time of the Seventeenth Congress in 1934 through 1953. However, there is a prior challenge, and that is the *personal* charisma *Lenin* possessed vis-à-vis his Bolshevik followers.

More than anyone, Robert Tucker has convincingly outlined the features of Lenin's personal charisma. In Tucker's words, "To be a Bolshevik in the early years was not so much to accept a particular set of beliefs as it was to gravitate into the orbit of Lenin as a political mentor, revolutionary strategist, and personality."[5] The Bolshevik colony in Geneva

> proved to be a group of people who regarded themselves as Lenin's disciples and were worshipful in their attitude towards him. Although he was then only 33 years old, they habitually referred to him as the "Old Man" (*starik*), thereby expressing profound respect for his Marxist erudition and his wisdom in all matters pertaining to revolution.[6]

Lenin's charismatic status was, of course, enhanced and confirmed by his personal role in the October Revolution. Tucker makes a very strong case for what he terms the "leader-centered movement."

Without denying the significance of Lenin's personal charisma or the extent to which Leninism was and remains a movement with strong leader orientations, I feel Tucker's argument is somewhat misleading. This is not because he fails to recognize elements in Lenin's behavior that are inconsistent with personal charisma, but rather because Tucker does not systematically relate Lenin's personal qualities to the defining features of the party he created.

In contrast, in a study of Lenin entitled "The Great Headmaster," Edmund Wilson has described Lenin in terms that are quite literally coincident with those we have used to describe his party. The core of Wilson's description is contained in the following passage:

> Though he [Lenin] was susceptible . . . to very strong personal attachments which survived political differences . . . [he] could no more allow these feelings to influence his political action than the headmaster can allow himself to be influenced in the matter of grades or discipline by his affection for a favorite pupil.[7]

In a society where personal attachments were an integral part of social organization, Lenin's detachment was culturally revolutionary. Furthermore, this personal detachment was placed in the service of a political organization that was designed to mirror his own qualities. In this light, Tucker's comments on Lenin's actions as party leader and in response to the growing cult of his person take on added

---

[5] Robert C. Tucker, ed., *The Lenin Anthology* (New York: W. W. Norton & Company, 1975), p. xlv.

[6] *Ibid.*

[7] Edmund Wilson, *To the Finland Station* (Garden City, N. Y.: Doubleday, 1953), p. 391.

meaning. According to Tucker, "As supreme leader, [Lenin] did not simply issue commands to the ruling group; he did not rule by arbitrary Diktat. Automatic acquiescence in his position was not expected."[8] And when Lenin became aware that he was being made the object of a personality cult, he responded negatively. He summoned one of his aides in the Council of People's Commissars and asked:

> What is this? How could one permit it? . . . They write that I'm such and such, exaggerate everything, call me a genius, a special kind of man. Why, this is horrible. . . . All our lives we have carried on an ideological struggle against the glorification of personality, of the individual. *We long ago solved the question of heroes.*[9]

Lenin's reference to the "question of heroes" should not be treated casually. There is a sense in which both Leninism and Nazism emphasize the heroic ethic. It is not in the appreciation of heroism that Leninism differs from Nazism; it is in the designation of the heroic agent. For Lenin, the Party is Hero[10]—not the individual leader. *The fact that Lenin possessed personal charisma is not as significant as the way in which he defined charisma and related it to the organization he created.* As an individual, he combined forceful charismatic certainty with a genuine and persistent emphasis on empirical and impersonal modes of investigation and interaction. His party was created (so to speak) in his own image. And that image was distinctive in its *novel recasting* of elements—heroism, arbitrariness, and absolute certainty, along with impersonal discipline, planning, and empirical investigation.

One might well remark that perhaps there was a novel recasting of such elements during Lenin's lifetime but certainly not after—not during the period of "high" Stalinism from the Seventeenth Congress in 1934 through 1953. As an observation, this remark is valuable; as a conclusion, it is superficial. In fact, an examination of Stalinism is the best way to point out the differences between Nazism and Leninism and single out the defining features of Leninism.

Certainly the formal similarities between Stalinism and the

---

[8]Tucker, *The Lenin Anthology*, p. lvi.

[9]*Ibid.*, p. lx.

[10]An article examining heroism as an integral component of Marxism-Leninism's conception of the cadre, the Party itself, the idealized character of the working class, and its images of post-capitalist society would be of great value.

Nazi regime are striking and by no means all superficial. The cult of the personality that surrounded Stalin (and has at times surrounded other Leninist leaders) was in a basic respect every bit as intense as that surrounding Hitler. *Even more significant than the cult of personality was the Stalinist "cult of cadres," captured in the saying "The cadres decide everything."* Under Stalinism the Party and regime organization might be viewed as no more than an aggregation of hierarchically ordered heroes—again quite like Nazi organization. These consequential similarities do indeed allow for and call for comparison. However, the comparison itself reveals a character-defining difference between Stalinist-Leninism and Nazism that is more important than the similarities.

In a relatively (and inexplicably) ignored article on factionalism in the Nazi Party, Joseph Nyomarkey has spelled out the difference between Stalinist-Leninism and Nazism quite well. Nyomarkey is intrigued by the fact that in Nazism there did not appear to be the same incidence or type of factionalism that appears in Leninism. His explanation is that there are two types of movements—charismatic and ideological. In the charismatic movement (i. e., Nazism), "the leader claims authority because he incorporates the idea in his person," while in the ideological movement (i. e., Stalinist-Leninism), "the leaders will claim authority on the basis of the dogma, and will always represent themselves as its representatives. . . ."[11] Nyomarkey goes on to argue that in an ideological movement it is the "dogma which ultimately holds the group together and which lends authority to the leader . . . [and] the dogma which can give rise to various interpretations which can in turn become the bases of factional conflicts."[12]

The point is crucial. It suggests that even under Stalin the formal or ideal basis of Leninist party organization, membership definition, and policy formulation was independent from his personal insight. *Can it be shown to have mattered?* In several ways. First, Stalin had difficulty in establishing a Führer position, whereas Nazism was defined precisely in terms of the Führerprinzip. Second, there is the opportunity *within the Leninist Party of a legitimate basis* for someone like Khrushchev to attack the "cult of person-

---

[11]Joseph Nyomarkey, "Factionalism in the National Socialist German Workers' Party, 1925-1926: The Myth and Reality of the 'Northern Faction,'" *Political Science Quarterly* LXXX, 1 (March 1965): 45.
[12]*Ibid.*

ality" *and* the notion that "cadres decide everything."[13] A third and even more telling piece of evidence has to do with a character-defining feature of Stalinism itself: the idea of a *"correct line."* An appreciation of the place and meaning of this notion in Leninism (and Stalinism as one expression of Leninism) goes a long way in helping to delineate the novelty of Leninism as a distinctive amalgam of charismatic and modern (i. e., impersonal, analytic, and empirical) elements.

At the Sixteenth Party Congress in 1930, Stalin addressed himself to the question of leadership. What—he asked—guaranteed that the Party would be an effective political organization? Was it the presence of a great leader? Someone privileged in his insight into the working of history? Stalin answered No. "For correct leadership by the Party it is necessary, apart from everything else, that the Party should have a correct line. . . ."[14] However, in 1930 Stalin had not yet attained the "sultanist" leadership that was to be his after 1934.[15] His comments at the Eighteenth Party Congress in 1939—at a time when his personal mastery of the Party was well established— thus have added importance. Stalin once again turned to the question of leadership and made the following critical statement:

> After a correct political line has been worked out and tested in practice, the Party cadres become the decisive force in the leadership. . . . *A correct political line is of course the primary and most important thing.*[16]

Let us now draw some conclusions about Leninist organization as a novel form of charisma—an instance of charismatic imper-

---

[13] George Breslauer emphasizes Khrushchev's critical stance toward the party cadres [*apparatchiks*] in "Khrushchev Reconsidered," *Problems of Communism* XXV, 5 (September-October 1976): 18-34.

[14] J. V. Stalin, "Political Report of the Central Committee to the Sixteenth Congress of the Communist Party of the Soviet Union (CPSU) (Bolshevik), June 27, 1930," in J. V. Stalin, *Works*, vol. 12 (April 1929-June 1930) (Moscow: Foreign Languages Publishing House, 1955; reprinted by Red Star Press Ltd., London, n. d.).

[15] More properly, "neo-sultanism," a variant of a neo-patrimonial political order in which the leader's personal (political) discretion is the political system's defining feature. Max Weber discusses the sultanist variant of patrimonialism in *Economy and Society*, vol. 1, pp. 231-32.

[16] J. V. Stalin, "Report to the Eighteenth Congress of the CPSU (Bolshevik) On the Work of the Central Committee," in *The Essential Stalin*, ed. Bruce Franklin (Garden City, N. Y.: Doubleday, 1972), pp. 373-74.

sonality. (1) Both Leninism and Nazism are in crucial respects instances of heroically oriented responses to the class order developments of Western Europe. (2) Both Lenin and Stalin possessed personal charisma, and particularly during Stalin's rule the leader threatened the Party as the primary locus of charisma. (3) Even under Stalin the emphasis on the leader and cadres—at least in formal and ideal terms—always remained subordinate to the Party as the agent capable of formulating a *correct line*, a program separate from the personal insight of the leader. (4) The emphasis on the primacy of a *correct line* strongly suggests that even when minor or latent, the charismatic impersonalism of the Party is an integral/defining component of Leninism that is constantly available in a formal sense—and intermittently available in a political sense—as a legitimate basis for countering tendencies toward Führerism. The Twentieth Party Congress is the most striking but by no means the only illustration of this point. (5) It is misleading to distinguish between charismatic and ideological movements à la Nyomarkey. Rather, one can distinguish different types of charismatic movements, with Leninism being one and Nazism another. The leader is charismatic in Nazism; the program and (possibly) the leader are charismatic in Leninism.[17]

The importance of the notion of the *correct line* in Leninism is that it is not a typical party program. Instead, it parallels the organizational character of the Party, itself an amalgam of modern and charismatic elements. The "correct line" is simultaneously an analytic and empirical statement of the stages of national and international development, a set of policy guides, *and* an authoritatively compelling and exclusive ideological-political statement that must be adopted and adhered to.

In the "correct line," one has a striking contemporary instance of a modern program encompassed and understood in neo-sacral terms. Clearly, at different points in the developmental history of Leninist regimes, the empirical-impersonal elements have been severely constrained. Gulag, Lysenko, and "Dizzy with Success"

[17] There is a constant tendency in Leninism toward strong *executive* leaders. This is not the same as a constant tendency toward the emergence of a *charismatic* leader, as in the case in Nazism, Fascism, or war bands. I would argue that it is possible to specify the developmental points at which the emergence of *charismatic* leadership in Leninist regimes is likely and when there is likely to be an attempt on the part of the Party elite to create a charismatic aura around a leader (a related but different phenomenon than the emergence of a charismatic leader).

THE LENINIST RESPONSE

cannot, should not, and *do not have to be* ignored to sustain our argument that Leninism is a conflictual but effective amalgam of charismatic impersonalism.

Lenin recast the mutually exclusive elements of individual heroism and impersonal modern organization in creating a "party of a new type." This party combined heroism and impersonalism, charismatic arbitrariness (i. e., antipathy toward rational procedures and calculations) and sober empirical examination of social change. No better formal expression of this novel amalgam can be found than the notion of the "correct line." However, the striking differences in the weighting and definition of charismatic and modern elements in the Lenin, Stalin, Khrushchev, and Brezhnev regimes make clear the need for a synthetic statement of the constants and variables in the syndrome of Leninist charismatic organization.

One can identify charismatic and modern imperatives in Leninist parties and regimes. These imperatives are *constant and conflictual*. They provide for a continuously recognizable identity alongside the historically varying and developmentally related features of Leninist organization.[18] On the charismatic side, there is the conception of the working class, cadres, and Party as heroic elements. In particular, the Party is called on to sacrifice, struggle, and exercise continual vigilance to maintain its purpose and commitment to the realization of historical laws of social development that are conceived in teleological and universal terms. On the modern side, there is a materialist orientation that (with varying degrees of effectiveness but undeniable persistence) calls for an empirical, non-dogmatic examination of social change and organization, as well as for the collective discussion of social issues.

In contrast to the constant elements of Leninism, there are variables whose identification can explain the changes in the institutional facade, policies, and ideological emphases that mark the *developmental profile* of Leninist regimes. Two are of particular im-

---

[18]To suggest the existence of organizational constants in Leninism is not to assert their "Platonic" imperviousness to the national and international environments with which Leninist regimes interact. Rather, the emphasis on the existence of organizationally constant imperatives directs one's attention to the types of situations Leninist regimes are likely to avoid, resist, and/or be unwilling/unable to adapt to. For a most impressive analysis of a nation's adaptation within the framework of ideological constants, see Louis Hartz, *The Liberal Tradition in America* (New York: Harcourt, Brace & World, 1955), *passim*.

portance. The first I term *developmental tasks*. For current purposes, it is crucial to understand that a Leninist elite's adoption of a specific task causes particular types of political uncertainties and, consequently, particular types of regime structures to manage those uncertainties.[19] These regime structures vary in terms of the relative power held by the Party leader and by the Party's central organs, the relative status of the Party vis-à-vis police and military institutions, the distinctive competence of the cadres who are recruited (i. e., in risk-taking, coercion, or social management), and the status of ideology, from that of partisan-empirical instrument to that of a stereotyped or dogmatic conception of reality.

The second variable is the *sociocultural milieu* within which a Leninist party and regime operates. Whether, to what extent, and in which areas a society is primarily status- or class-oriented and organized will significantly shape the way in which Leninist leadership is expressed, policies are implemented, authority is interpreted, and so on.

To summarize: The profile of a Leninist regime at any given point reflects both the interplay of organizational constants— charismatic (heroic) and modern (materialist) elements—and of these constant-conflictual imperatives with varying developmental tasks and changes in the sociocultural configuration of the society being acted upon. To point out the complexity of this relationship would be trite. Whether a phenomenon is simple or complex is rarely the crucial consideration. It is whether we can make the phenomenon intelligible. The terms and mode of analysis presented here increase that possibility if in no other way than by not confusing organizationally constant with developmentally specific elements in the Leninist syndrome.[20]

---

[19]See Jowitt, "Inclusion and Mobilization in European Leninist Regimes," pp. 69-71.

[20]While valuable in other respects, both Richard Lowenthal's "Development vs. Utopia in Communist Policy," in *Change in Communist Systems*, ed. Chalmers Johnson (Stanford: Stanford University Press, 1970), pp. 33-117, and Robert C. Tucker's "The Deradicalization of Marxist Movements," in Tucker, *The Marxian Revolutionary Idea*, pp. 172-215, contribute to this confusion. (Along with my criticism of these two works, I very readily acknowledge how much Lowenthal and Tucker have shaped my own interests.) Other influential studies in the field present a unidimensional or "collapsed" view of development in Soviet and Soviet-type regimes—for example, Samuel P. Huntington, "Social and Institutional Dynamics of One-Party Systems," in *Authoritarian Politics in Modern Society*, eds. S. P. Huntington and Clement H. Moore (New York:

THE LENINIST RESPONSE

One highly significant aspect of Leninism as a type of charismatic organization remains to be examined—i. e., its status or traditional features. Once this is done, we shall have a more complete grasp of Leninism as an effective institutional substitute in some peasant countries with a non-feudal legacy for the type of class organization and identification that emerged in nineteenth-century Western Europe—a substitute that in certain respects "fits" and in others attacks the institutional and cultural profile of a status society.

To develop an argument about the status or traditional features of Leninist charismatic organization requires a summation and extension of Weber's observations about the relationship between tradition and charisma. According to Weber, charisma and tradition are fundamentally antithetical. Charisma calls for revolution; tradition, for conservation. However, in certain formal respects, traditional and charismatic orientations are similar, given their stress on personal (not abstract) and substantive (not formal) considerations. Both forms of social action are "hostile" to the impersonal-rational calculation that typifies modern organization. In Weber's words, "the two basically antagonistic forces of charisma and tradition regularly merge with one another; . . . the external forms of the two structures of domination are . . . often similar to the point of being identical."[21]

Identifying the *formal overlap* that exists between charismatic and status (or traditional) orientations is an important step in coming to grips with the ability of Leninism to operate effectively in a peasant-status milieu, but alone it is inadequate. Two other aspects of the charisma-tradition relationship—that to the best of my knowledge Weber did not develop—are highly consequential for a charismatic leader's (or organization's) political effectiveness. *First*, charismatic leaders or organizations *gain entry* into the very societies they wish to destroy and transform by possessing traditional features that are *formally* congruent with certain facets of a peasant-status society. (We shall enumerate these features below.) A charismatic leader is unlikely to get the majority of a society to adhere to his vision for the simple reason that by definition his vision is revolu-

---

Basic Books, 1970), pp. 3-48, and Zbigniew Brzezinski, "The Soviet Political System: Transformation or Degeneration?," in *Dilemmas of Change in Soviet Politics*, ed. Z. Brzezinski (New York: Columbia University Press, 1969), pp. 1-35.

[21] M. Weber, *Economy and Society*, vol. 3, esp. p. 1122.

tionary and entails fundamental revisions in the identity and organization of individuals and groups. Yet charismatic leaders have adherents. The standard explanation from Weber through Deutsch has focused on social mobilization and turbulence.[22] A society subject to serious disruption, stress, and uncertainty creates a pool of persons available for recommitment. This is a valuable and empirically confirmable point; however, there is more to it. What makes the charismatic effective is not only the availability of socially mobilized clusters, but also the charismatic leader's (and/or organization's) *possession of qualities that at least in a formal or structural sense are consistent with the defining features of the very society he (or it) wishes to transform. It is the possession of these features that gives the charismatic entry into the society he wishes to change.*

Let us refer to the examples of charisma we discussed earlier: Christ lived at a time of great turmoil (i. e., social mobilization) in Israel, but it was his status as a rabbi and student of Mosaic law that made him intelligible to others, gained him an audience, and gave him a toehold into the society he wished to transform. It was Hitler's patriotic participation in the German army in World War I and his credentials as a German nationalist and supporter of the German army that provided him with a base in a society that he wished to transform in ways that many a nationalist would rue.

Lenin's case would appear to be more difficult to interpret in these terms. He was by no stretch of the imagination a Russian nationalist (as, in a peculiar fashion, Stalin was). But he *did* present himself in terms that were intelligible to a "mobilized" Russian audience. Not only was he considered "the old man" by his followers, but also his self-presentation in critical respects obviously conformed to that role, as did his more general disposition, which Wilson captured with his notion of Lenin the headmaster. Wilson's comment that Lenin "had to have loyal adherents, with whom he could actually work . . . and [that] there appeared in his relation to his group something of the attitude of the older brother, carried over from his relation to his family, and a good deal of the inspired schoolmaster"[23] suggests that while Lenin was no Russian nationalist, he was —in identifiable sociocultural respects—a Russian.

Second, a charismatic's traditional features *mediate* between an organization with revolutionary commitments and its need to

[22]See Deutsch, pp. 493-514.
[23]Wilson, p. 390.

recruit members from a population *which, even if socially mobilized, still culturally orients itself in terms of status (or traditional) orientations and expectations.*[24] When Lenin said, "We can (and must) begin to build socialism, not with abstract human material, or with human material specially prepared by us, but with the human material bequeathed to us by capitalism,"[25] he might also have observed that the distinctiveness of his party's organization and orientation was its ability (under certain conditions) to offer itself as an intelligible medium *for the recruitment and transformation of* that "imperfect" material.

A case in point and one that can be used to demonstrate the utility of looking at the relationship between charisma and tradition in the terms we have devised is the success of the Chinese Communist Party in recruiting adherents during the Japanese invasion.

In his important works on peasant nationalism, Johnson has argued that there was a direct relationship between the social mobilization of the Chinese peasants and the consequent opportunity for the Chinese Communist Party to provide uprooted peasants with new national-political identities. I suggest this relationship is stated a bit mechanically. In light of our argument about the relationship between charisma and tradition, we would hypothesize that in a situation of intense social disruption, the Chinese Communist Party was successful in recruiting large numbers of adherents in part because as an organization it contained a number of features that were at least formally or structurally congruent with a number of the defining features of a peasant-status society. The formal status features of the Chinese Communist Party's Leninist organization mediated between its charismatic-revolutionary and national commitments and the status orientations of the socially mobilized mass base from which it had to recruit.[26]

---

[24]*Too often it is uncritically assumed that to be uprooted from an institutional setting is to be stripped of one's cultural orientations. A distinction should be made between social and cultural mobilization:* Typically, the latter lags behind the former. The difference in the extent of social and cultural mobilization within a given group may have a direct bearing on the types of organizations and appeals that are politically effective with that group.

[25]V. I. Lenin, "Left-Wing Communism—An Infantile Disorder," in V. I. Lenin, *Collected Works* (Moscow: Progress Publishers, 1966), vol. 31 (April-December 1920), p. 50.

[26]See Chalmers A. Johnson: *Peasant Nationalism and Communist Power* (Stanford: Stanford University Press, 1962), *passim*, and "Peasant Nationalism Revisited: The Biography of a Book," *China Quarterly*, December 1977, p. 774.

It is now possible to provide a final characterization of Leninism: The distinctive quality of Leninist organization is the enmeshment of status (traditional) and class (modern) elements in the framework of an impersonal-charismatic organization.

The status-like features (that at times are so consequential as mediating elements in the process of recruitment) include the following: (a) a marked tendency to distinguish between insiders (i. e., members of the Party) and outsiders; (b) an emphasis on the security and protection of belonging to a closed, well-bounded group; and (c) a placement of power in the hands of cadres whose central *personal* role is emphasized—particularly during the initial developmental phases of Leninist regimes.

These status-like features—we have hypothesized—make a Leninist party *intelligible* to some sectors of a peasant population. *They do not necessarily or automatically make it politically acceptable or influential.* Its *influence* depends *not* on the formal correspondence of certain of its features with those of peasant society, but on the level of social mobilization in a society *and* on whether there exist rival radical organizations whose *substantive* commitments are more aligned with those of a peasant population. To take the Romanian case as one in point: nativist nationalist movements of a charismatic order, such as the Iron Guard, in addition to an organizational format that was consistent with peasant orientations, had a set of substantive (religious and cultural) commitments closely related to the peasants' own; thus membership in a group like the Iron Guard involved much less of an identity shift for a peasant than if he were to join the Communist Party with its materialist (modern) emphases.[27]

This discussion leads us to a fundamental hypothesis: *Leninism's novelty as a political organization rests in significant measure with the fact that its traditional features are more structural than substantive in nature.* One test of this hypothesis is that peasants who are recruited into a Leninist party should initially find much of its organization and orientation intelligible rather than alien. But

---

Obviously, the Party's mediating role was more central to those peasants who joined the Party than to the larger number of non-Party peasant soldiers and followers, who probably held a more complicated view of national identity than Johnson suggests.

[27] For those interested in the Romanian case, I develop this point in K. Jowitt, *Revolutionary Breakthroughs and National Development* (Berkeley: University of California Press, 1971), pp. 85-89.

after joining, they should become aware of organizational features of a substantive order that not only do not coincide with peasant social organization and orientation, but also actively oppose them. As we shall see below, there is supportive evidence for this hypothesis.[28]

The organizational features of Leninism that oppose peasant social organization are the Party's class or modern commitments. They include an emphasis on the individual responsibility of members for the execution of tasks, achievement as a central criterion for mobility and recognition, and—consequent to the relationship between personal effort and organizational-social mobility—the development of a sense of personal-individual efficacy and control over events. The Party also emphasizes a more empirical, less magical appreciation of social and political problems. In fact, the argument can be made that *in societies and cultures where personal, discrete, and ritualistic orientations predominate, the potential significance and power of "scientific socialism" are precisely in the emphasis it places on empirical, abstract, and critical modes of investigation of and orientation to social phenomena.* Thus Dobrogeanu-Gherea's repeated emphasis that neo-serfdom was a systemic phenomenon—not the result of individually evil landlords—was a cultural break of epistemological and ontological proportions *insufficient* to bring about a social revolution but a *significant component* of such.

To stop at the point where one identifies a set of modern action orientations in the Leninist concept of organization and membership would be premature, misleading, and inconsistent with the theoretical approach of this work, however. To capture the distinctive quality of the class or modern features of Leninist parties and regimes, one has to specify their definition at an institutional—not social action—level. *It is the enmeshment of modern (and traditional) orientations in a novel type of charismatic framework that determines the manner in which these modern action orientations express themselves.* The charismatically impersonal features of Leninist organization are not simply neutral auspices under which modern developments of a Western-liberal order occur. Rather, they constrain and shape the modes of modern or class developments. *Thus individualism is expressed in the neo-corporate unit of the collective* (i. e., Party cell, work collective); achievement as a premise and

---

[28]For example, Pye's interviews with Malayan ex-guerillas (Lucian Pye, *Guerilla Communism in Malaya* [Princeton: Princeton University Press, 1956]).

imperative is in continual tension with the charismatic premise of Party membership as an heroic intrinsic quality; and scientific socialism as an emphasis on empirical, abstract, and critical orientations conflicts with the conception of scientific socialism as a grasp of inexorable, universal, and unilinear historical laws.

The Leninist party and regime is a novel package of charismatic, traditional, and modern elements, a recasting of the definition and relation of these three elements in such a way that the Party *combines impersonal and affective elements*[29] *and appeals effectively if not logically to some persons and groups in a turbulent society who themselves are a composite of heroic, status, and secular orientations.*[30]

Is there any empirical support for the argument that Leninism's novelty lies in its recasting of status and class elements under charismatic impersonal auspices? At the elite level, support for this argument comes from an examination of Ho Chi Minh's attraction to Leninism. At the mass level, there is interview data from Pye's seminal (and for some reason largely forgotten) study of Malayan ex-guerillas.

From Ho Chi Minh's various statements about Leninism, one can identify a set of central perceptions. First, one is struck by Ho's

---

[29] In this sense, the Leninist party can be seen as the formal organizational equivalent of Japanese social organization. As spelled out by Nakane, the distinctiveness of Japanese social organization rests on the fusion of affective and hierarchical-organizational elements. Unlike other peasant societies, in traditional Japanese society, the organization, not the family, has been the object of identity and loyalty (see Chie Nakane, *Japanese Society* [Berkeley: University of California Press, 1970], esp. pp. 1-7 and 40-63).

[30] Three considerations are relevant in connection with the reference to "some persons and groups": (1) The number of people in a peasant society both institutionally uprooted and (for whatever reasons) oriented to empirical, analytic, and impersonal conceptions and practices is likely to be relatively small. (2) These people are not simply peasants, but rather "composites" of status, charismatic, and secular orientations. In most cases they are the products of a peasant milieu, and (with exceptions) they are less mobilized culturally than socially. (3) The majority of those adhering to the Party at any given time is unlikely to be the "composite" type I refer to. For the majority, the decision to join the Party is likely to be based more on the absence of alternatives, decisions made by "significant others," career considerations, and so on. "Composite" types are more likely to be found within the influential cadre stratum. Pye, Hinton (*Fanshen* [New York: Vintage Books, 1966]), and Burks (*The Dynamics of Communism in Eastern Europe* [Princeton: Princeton University Press, 1961]) provide data that support this suggestion.

admiration of Lenin.[31] This admiration is significant in two respects. To begin with, there was the traditional—and in this case mediating—dimension of Ho's seeing Lenin as a political "elder" and hero. Subsequently, Ho's personal admiration of Lenin developed into an appreciation of the novel quality of heroism in Lenin*ism*—its incorporation of impersonal and empirical orientations. In an article for *Pravda* entitled "Leninism and the Liberation of Oppressed Peoples," Ho identified Lenin's contribution as twofold:

Lenin helped the working people . . . to realize in a more comprehensive manner *the laws of social development*, the requirements and *objective conditions* of the political struggle *in every stage of the . . . revolution* . . . . He gave [the oppressed masses] the *miraculous weapon* to fight for their emancipation—the theory and tactics of Bolshevism.[32]

In Ho's eyes, Lenin had created an organization—the Bolshevik Party—that combined the heroic (i. e., the "miraculous weapon") and the scientific (i. e., the "laws of social development"). It was this *novel recasting* of familiar appeals in substantively new formats and unfamiliar appeals in formally familiar guises that distinguished Leninism. For example, heroism (a familiar appeal) was related to an impersonal-formal organization (an unfamiliar format), while ideological support of anti-colonialism, national equality, and political activism for the masses (unfamiliar appeals) were related to an authoritarian organization with a charismatic leader (a familiar format). It was this novel recasting that appealed to those like Ho who were themselves composites of status, charismatic, and secular orientations.

Ho saw Lenin as the "great leader [who] after having liberated his own people wanted to liberate other peoples, too." But he also saw that Lenin, unlike a traditional "big man," had "mapped out a definite program" to reach his goals.[33] And this program was ideally based as much on empirical analysis and critical theory as on conventional observation or inspiration. In short, for Ho, Lenin was a "big man," but a "big man of a new type."

To be sure, this is not an exhaustive explanation of Ho Chi Minh's commitment to Leninism, and it is a single case. But it is a

---

[31]Bernard B. Fall, ed., *Ho Chi Minh on Revolution: Selected Writings, 1920-66* (New York: Praeger, 1967), pp. 23-24, 39-40, 61-62.
[32]*Ibid.*, pp. 255-56.
[33]*Ibid.*, p. 39.

highly significant case, and the fit between our identification of what is novel in Leninism and Ho's perception of Leninism's distinctiveness is not forced.

At the mass level, Pye's interview data from Malayan ex-guerillas are remarkably consistent with our argument about Leninism. (That these findings have not been given the sustained attention they deserve is probably in part due to the absence of a conceptual statement about Leninism which would indicate their general significance.) According to Pye,

> In contrast to the impersonal relations of the . . . competitive labor market that had threatened [the ex-guerillas'] sense of security before they joined the party, they felt that they had *discovered in Communism the highly personal relations they craved*, [but] *they learned that behind the facade of personal intimacy lay the impersonal rationale of the party.* . . . They discovered that in actual fact they were socially isolated within the party.[34]

In his very interesting discussion of comradeship and friendship in China, Vogel also supports our notion of the Party as a substitute form of impersonality—a charismatic impersonalism of discipline and affectivity.[35] Vogel's purpose is "to explore the decline of friendliness and the rise of comradeship."[36] The exploration comes up with the following discoveries. First, comradeship as a form of social interaction is more limited than friendship, engaging less of the total personality. It is more impersonal and formal—i. e., ideally it is oriented to impersonal roles, not their incumbents. It involves the creation of a standardized public mode of interaction between equals, in contrast to unique relations among bounded groups of friends. In short, comradeship is a form of social market where the "goods"—i. e., persons (rather than commodities)—are interchangeable, thereby increasing the combinatorial freedom and level of power available to the Party and state.

Second, the means used by the Chinese Communist Party to foster comradeship over friendship were to increase the fear of con-

[34]Pye, pp. 279-80; see also pp. 311-14.

[35]Ezra Vogel, "From Friendship to Comradeship: The Change in Personal Relations in Communist China," *China Quarterly*, no. 2 (January-March 1965): 1-28.

[36]*Ibid.*, p. 46. The language used below in summarizing Vogel's argument is my own. Vogel does not refer to a "standardized public mode of interaction," "social markets," or "combinatorial power." However, I do not think this language is inconsistent with the meaning of his argument.

fiding too closely in one's friends; the Party did so by creating mutual distrust and consequent social distance. Emotion and affect were to be redirected toward the Party and away from one's social acquaintances and personal friends. How different this sounds from the descriptions by Western social scientists of the capacity for mutual trust that was supposedly such an integral part of the West's unique developmental accomplishments! But was it? Certainly if one gives some weight to the role of Calvinism as a mode of social organization and orientation in the development of Western capitalism, one has to think twice. Calvinism argues adamantly for trust in God (equivalent to the Leninist Party), but according to Weber, "especially in the English Puritan literature [Calvinism argues] against any trust in the aid or friendship of men."[37] In both the English and Chinese cases, the significance of such a social orientation in a status society based on corporate identity is clear and revolutionary. *It creates "isolated" individuals, undermines the integrity of corporate social organization, and substitutes impersonal frames of reference that coordinate and standardize the actions of diverse people. Not trust, but impersonal, common organizational frames of reference are integral parts of modern development.*[38] The Leninist and Liberal modes differ significantly precisely with respect to the auspices under which the new mode of impersonalism developed. In the English case, impersonalism as an authoritative public norm developed in good measure (though by no means exclusively) through an internalized voluntary charismatic ideology, while in the Chinese and other Leninist cases, it has developed through the authoritative imposition of a charismatic organization.[39]

[37] M. Weber, *The Protestant Ethic*, p. 106.

[38] There is some empirical support for our contention. In his recent work, *Becoming Modern* (Cambridge, Mass.: Harvard University Press, 1974), Alex Inkeles notes that "there were some personal attributes which the theory . . . had identified as presumably part of the syndrome of individual modernity, but which nevertheless failed to legitimate their claim in our empirical investigation. . . . *For example, modern men evidently are not outstanding in trust*" (p. 117).

[39] As Weber noted about the creation of industries, "The mercantilistic regulations of the State might develop industries, but not, or certainly not alone, the spirit of capitalism; where they assumed a despotic authoritarian character, they to a large extent directly hindered it. . . . Thus a similar effect might well have resulted from ecclesiastical regimentation when it became excessively despotic. It enforced a particular type of external conformity, but in some cases weakened the subjective motives of rational conduct" (M. Weber, *The Protestant Ethic*,

There is additional information from Pye's Malayan study about the combining and recasting within the Party of traditional and modern elements under the auspices of an heroic charismatic organization. Pye's interviews suggested to him that for many ex-guerillas the Party was a route (the first in their experience) to mobility based on personal achievement, a route that gave them a sense of individual efficacy.[40] At the same time, they found the hierarchical organization of the Party quite consistent with their previous social and cultural experiences. However, they ran into confusion when they came up against the distinctive features of Leninist organization— charismatic impersonalism. The ex-guerillas responded to the personal authority of leading cadres in quite traditional terms, but they were often perplexed when cadres with whom they had formed what they thought to be typical status-personal relations criticized them for not having achieved certain *organizational* goals and even purged them on this basis.

While no comparable empirical studies of the Romanian Workers' Party (CP) have been undertaken, a partial "substitute" for such may be found in an organizational comparison with the other Romanian revolutionary movement during the interwar period—the Iron Guard. Both the Guard and the Party emphasized hierarchy and discipline of cadres. Both attempted to insulate their cadres from the contaminating effects of society. Both had supranational referents—one religious, the other ideological. Both argued the need for fundamental cultural transformation, not simply elite change.

Eugen Weber, who has written the most sophisticated analyses of interwar Romania, has suggested that for both the right and the left "the sources of dissatisfaction were similar, the radical conclusions were similar, *only the directions* in which people follow their conclusions were different, and even these were essentially a combination of populism and sectarian elitism.[41] Similarities between the Iron Guard and the Party did exist; however, what Weber describes as "only the directions" is exactly where the qualitative differences between the Guard and Party lay.

p. 152). Analagously, there are different routes to a class society based on the individual and impersonal norms of action, but different routes ensure that class societies will vary in ethos and operation.

[40]Pye, pp. 316, 318.

[41]E. Weber: "The Men of the Archangel," *Journal of Contemporary History* 1, 1 (1966): 124, and "Romania."

THE LENINIST RESPONSE

For the Guard, a charismatic leader was *the* central ideological feature, both in theory and in practice; not so for the Party. In the Guard, songs were favored over speeches—i. e., the Guard's emphasis was on form, externality, ritual, and magic, while the Party's was a more analytic orientation to social issues. In the Guard men counted and programs were disdained, while in the Party the emphasis on cadres was integrally related to the formulation of a "correct line."[42] The Guard's symbolic references were the King and People— an almost paradigmatic status relationship (personal and hierarchical).[43] The Party's major referent was class. Even the terms for the

---

[42] As is well known, the line was anything but "correct" in many respects. The Romanian party's line was authoritatively set by Stalin, often in ignorance of Romanian conditions and without regard for the Romanian party's own political interests. While significant for certain issues, this point is relevant at a different level of analysis and does not contradict the one we are making in our comparison of the Romanian CP and the Iron Guard.

[43] The usual comparative reference for the Iron Guard movement has been European fascism (though Eugen Weber has suggestively pointed to the millenarian-syncretist movements of sub-Saharan Africa for comparison). I suggest that the Guard might be more fruitfully compared with the Moslem Brotherhood movement in Egypt during the interwar period. The points of similarity are impressive. Both movements were dependent on a charismatic leader (Codreanu for the Guard and al-Banna for the Brotherhood), and neither ever really recovered after that leader's death. Both movements were embedded in religious idioms and frameworks, each reflecting the different content of the respective religions; for example, one does not find in the Brotherhood the emphasis on death which there was in the Guard. Both emphasized absolute discipline and obedience without any pretext of criticism/self-criticism or "debate before obedience." Both demonstrated a reluctance to take power (at least until Codreanu's death in the case of the Guard), and never effectively resolved their "educative" orientation with that of programmatic leadership. The revolutionary thrust of both movements was deflected by their allegiance to the King, and both were consequently disarmed quite easily. Both defined membership and organization in a fashion that emphasized affective-personal allegiances rather than affective-impersonal ones—a limited but interesting indication being the Brotherhood's designation of its membership units as "usra," a term highly congruent with the Guard's use of the term "nest." In the composition of both movements, one sees the predominance of the same social types— particularly at the elite-activist levels. Students, clerks, civil servants, and teachers are found in large numbers—"those who had passed through varying degrees of Westernization and had already accepted some of its premises," but who for material and ideal reasons were still attached to traditional religious and cultural frames of reference. Similarities in the respective positions and roles of Premier Brătianu in Romania and Zaghlul in Egypt, the Liberal Party and Wafd, the position of the monarchy in each country, the role of the army and that of the Great Powers—all add structural plausibility to a comparative study. (On

THE LENINIST RESPONSE TO NATIONAL DEPENDENCY

basic membership units in each organization highlight the parties' different characters (ethos as much as structure): in the Guard, the basic unit was the "nest"; in the Party, the "cell."

What emerges from these contrasts between the Guard and the Party is the difference in quality—not degree—that characterizes Leninism as a "direction" or response to conditions in a dependent peasant country.

There is another major element of Leninism, along with its substitution of charismatic for procedural impersonalism and its recasting of status and class features under charismatic organizational auspices. Leninism as a mode of analysis and strategy is based on an "ingenious error."

In his *General Economic History*, Weber referred to the "old truth . . . that an ingenious error is more fruitful for science than stupid accuracy."[44] With due modification, one could argue that Leninism as a particular approach to social change in a peasant country is founded on an "ingenious error." This error is the incorrect extrapolation of certain social distinctions from the economic differentiation Leninists observe in peasant society.

It was Schumpeter who pointed out the reductionist synthesis in Marxism of social and economic elements. Schumpeter argued for the autonomy of the social dimension and for recognizing the *social* character of classes. For him, classes were made of families, not atomized individuals whose life chances were determined by their relation to the means of production.[45]

Shanin's study of the Russian peasant village extends and confirms, so to speak, Schumpeter's conception of social organization. Shanin found that Russian villages at the time of collectivization were vertically integrated units in which *economic differentials existed but were not the primary dimension along which a community was organized.*[46] Rather, a village community was made up of peasant family households that experienced generational cyclical

---

the Moslem Brotherhood, see in particular Richard P. Mitchell, *The Society of the Muslim Brothers* [London: Oxford University Press, 1969], *passim*. On the Guard, see the references in E. Weber: "The Men of the Archangel" and "Romania.")

[44]M. Weber, *General Economic History*, p. 30.

[45]Joseph A. Schumpeter, *Capitalism, Socialism and Democracy* (New York: Harper & Row, 1962), pp. 9-20.

[46]Shanin, *passim*.

mobility—a phenomenon that favored vertical integration rather than class antagonism. Shanin's description of Russian villagers united around the village kulaks in opposition to the "kombedy" and Red Army very much resembles the recent solidary village responses to efforts at *vijijini ujamaa* (collectivization) in Tanzania.[47]

In short, theoretical argument and empirical investigation seem to support the populist-nationalist idea that in peasant society, economic differences do not signify that class is the primary basis of identification and conflict. The Leninist analysis of village organization is in error—not in pointing to social distinctions, but in conceiving them to be class (rather than status) distinctions. But the error— murderous in the Soviet case for several reasons, including the fact that much time had elapsed between land reform and collectivization, and the fact that land reform itself had not been accomplished by a regime with a strong rural party apparatus (as in China)[48]—

---

[47]"Kombedy" were committees of poor peasants. The original kombedy movement occurred during the Russian Civil War. The committees were revitalized during collectivization.

In *Smolensk Under Soviet Rule*, Fainsod provides some data on the tendency of poor and middle peasants to unite with kulaks against the regime's collectivization efforts: "Of the 122 persons who were apprehended in October (1929, the Western Oblast) for committing 'terrorist' acts, approximately half were kulaks and well to do peasants, and another 45% were middle and poor peasants. The latter group, observed the procurator, was closely allied with the kulak elements by 'family and economic ties' and still manifested a 'petty-bourgeois' ideology" (p. 241).

On the response to collectivization in Dodoma, Tanzania, see Frances Hill, "Ujamaa: African Socialist Productionism in Tanzania," in *Socialism in the Third World*, eds. Helen Desfosses and Jacques Levesque (New York: Praeger, 1975), esp. pp. 237-45. Hill stresses that "those with little land were as insistent [i. e., opposed to collectivization] as those with more to lose" (p. 241). On the other hand, Issa G. Shivji, a Leninist, holds to the expected position that in Iringa, another region in Tanzania where collectivization was opposed, "the poor and the middle peasants remain politically dominated and economically exploited" (*Class Struggles in Tanzania* [New York: Monthly Review Press, 1976], p. 108). It is true that Iringa is economically more developed than Dodoma. However, I remain skeptical that even in Iringa the peasants see themselves primarily in economic class and exploitation terms. That there are tensions and conflicts in Iringa and Dodoma and in every peasant region is obvious to anyone who has had occasion to observe village life. To invariably interpret them in economic class terms can be misleading.

[48]On China's land reform, see the excellent piece by Thomas P. Bernstein, "Leadership and Mass Mobilization in the Soviet and Chinese Collectivization Campaigns of 1929-1930 and 1955-1956: A Comparison," *China Quarterly* 31 (July-September 1967): 1-47.

is "ingenious." The ideological-conceptual map with which Leninists work leads them to see economic differences as evidences of social polarization and the existence of "class allies" in the villages, *and it enables them to do politically what nationalists can do only analytically*—i. e., distinguish and oppose competing social bases and conceptions of the nation-state (e. g., working class vs. middle class nation). Working with such a paradigm, Leninists attack the institutional bases, not simply the elite organization of peasant society.

The Leninist "error" leads to *collectivization—an attack on the sociocultural bases of peasant institutional life, not (simply) to land reform—an attack on the political economy of elite organization in a peasant society.*[49] The "right" targets are attacked for the "wrong" reasons. Not simply elites, but the basic institutions of a status society—the peasant corporate household and the village community—are broken through—not eliminated, but decisively transformed and given new roles in the social, economic, and political order.

An attack on *institutions* is the condition for breaking out of the pattern of "arrested development" characteristic of peasant countries.[50] In Communist countries, the attack has typically taken the form of substituting organizational for social elites and formal organizations (e. g., the collectives) for social modes of economic production (e. g., the peasant village household). Organizational cadres do not necessarily displace village status figures ("big men," "patrons," "patriarchs") from affective and informal roles, *but they do replace them in authoritative (political and economic) roles*. Similarly, the collectives undermine the peasant households and village communities as institutions and models of social, economic, and political power more than as work units or informal social referents. The kulak is *not* an alien in the village who is seen primarily as an economic exploiter, but he is a key figure in the cor-

---

[49]David Mitrany's *Marx Against the Peasant: A Study in Social Dogmatism* (New York: Collier Books, 1961) has long been considered a classic analysis of Leninism's relation to the peasantry. Yet in light of our discussion of the Leninist response to agrarian society, Mitrany's observations take on quite different meanings from those he assigns to his remarks about Leninism's artificial relationship to the revolutionary process in China and East Europe and from what he considers to be Marxism's unnecessary and misguided opposition to the peasants.

[50]Our thesis is that any successful attempt to decisively change the structure and ethos of a peasant-status society depends on institutional, not simply elite change. Leninism is one ideological-organizational and strategic means of doing this in peasant societies *at certain levels of social and economic development*.

porate household and village system of social identification, organization, and power. Leninism errs in its understanding of his character and role, but it does so in a way that leads to strategies and policies that undermine the kulak, the peasant household, and the village community as defining institutions in a peasant-status society.

In historical retrospect, it might well be argued that taken on a grand scale, the distinctive feature of Leninist programs of social change has been the substitution of the individual for the corporate group as the social and cultural base of social action and identification, and that this feat was accomplished by replacing the peasant household with the peasant nuclear family through collectivization (and accompanying industrialization and education).

That in Communist countries the *institutional expression of individualism differs significantly* from its Western counterpart is predictable in terms of our analysis. The point here is that collectivization as the strategic manifestation of Lenin's "ingenious error" has a sociocultural as well as an economic significance.

The proverbial wisdom about collectivization is well illustrated by a comment by Brzezinski that Leninism is inapplicable to African conditions. According to Brzezinski, "a continuing Communist problem is the universal Communist failure in the agricultural sector, a failure that becomes especially embarrassing in dealing with a continent that is primarily agrarian."[51] Brzezinski's error is far from ingenious. He has confused agricultural and agrarian problems—or, in the terms used in this analysis, political-economic with sociocultural problems.[52]

Collectivization is more than an effort to economically and politically undermine landlords and kulaks; it is more than an effort to industrialize. It is an attack on the social institutions and cultural orientations of peasant society. To quote Roberts on the Romanian land reform of 1945: "The Communists undoubtedly exaggerated the *economic* importance of the boyars and the extent of their holdings. Nevertheless, a *certain boyar spirit* still prevailed in Ru-

---

[51]Brzezinski, "Conclusion: The African Challenge," in *Africa and the Communist World*, ed. Z. Brzezinski (Stanford: Stanford University Press, 1965), p. 210.

[52]Interestingly enough, a Danish expert called to Romania in the interwar period to review its rural problems emphasized that the problems were agrarian rather than agricultural (see Roberts, p. 63).

mania and the fact of land ownership continued to be a mark of prestige."[53]

Nothing that has been said thus far is meant to imply that Leninism and collectivization (industrialization) are the only means of bringing about significant changes in a peasant country. The reformist political economy analyses and strategies of Bukharin, Ataturk, Indira Gandhi, or the Ford Foundation *do* significantly alter the social organization of a peasant country. Reformist strategies *do* seriously modify the character of the peasant household through commercialization and *do* bring about major revisions in the state's role.[54] However, these strategies tend to be more sectoral than national in application (if not in rhetoric) and generally more oriented to changes in elite than in institutional patterns.[55] The neomercantilist state-society that emerges from such changes continues to be based on a highly personalistic, stereotyped, and fragmented division of labor. Because of the absence of a nationally effective framework of impersonal norms that institutionally standardize human and economic resources, thereby allowing for their greater mobility and interchange, there is a high degree of (social) resource immobilization and fragmentation.

It is important to recognize that with Leninist modes of development as well there is stereotyping and immobilization of certain types of resources at points in their developmental history, and in some respects unintentional reinforcement of certain status orientations among the population.[56] The differences between a reformist political economy approach and a revolutionary sociocultural one are not absolute. But an observation of this order tends to be more placating than discriminating: while the differences are not absolute, they are basic. The two types of strategies differ in their

---

[53]*Ibid.*, p. 299.

[54]In this connection, see Leys, chs. 5-8. The example of India is even more striking.

[55]The difference between regimes that initiate some type of land reform and those that follow collectivization-industrialization is quite striking with regard to the effective penetration and integration of the rural areas with the urban (see Jowitt, *Revolutionary Breakthroughs and National Development*, pp. 7-69).

[56]I have examined this process in Romania and have attempted to conceptualize it in K. Jowitt, "An Organizational Approach to the Study of Political Culture in Marxist-Leninist Systems," *American Political Science Review* LXVIII, 3 (September 1974): 1171-91.

impact on the central units of a peasant society—the extended household and village. Specifically, they differ in their ability to incorporate these units into a *national* political framework that is *effectively* based on impersonal norms of social action. The accomplishment of Leninism in a peasant society is that it authoritatively establishes a charismatic (not legal) type of impersonal institutional framework at all levels and in all sectors of society.

Developments during the NEP period in the Soviet Union highlight the relative incapacity of a reformist political economy approach to decisively recast a status society into a class society.

Bukharin, the leading proponent of what is here referred to as a reformist or political economy view, failed to see (as Pethybridge has so correctly noted) that under the auspices of the NEP, Nepmen, kulaks, and "kustarnyi," far from "growing into" socialism, were successfully using the new organizational formats introduced by the Party to expand and protect the social and cultural features of a kin-based, notable-ruled, corporately organized social order.[57] Bukharin held that due to the changes in the rural *elite* brought about by *land reform*, the *urban sector* (the cities) could act as "commanding heights" for the rural areas; this notion was put to the test and came up short.

Massell's study of Soviet transformation efforts in Central Asia during the 1920's provides striking evidence of the Sisyphus-like quality of social change strategies in a peasant country that emphasizes elite reorganization more than institutional transformation. According to Massell,

> It would appear that the separation of traditional leaders from their followers, even when successfully carried out ... did not ... automatically lead to a community's dissolution.[58]

---

[57]See Robert Pethybridge, *The Social Prelude to Stalinism* (London: The Macmillan Press, 1974), pp. 196-242, for an acute appraisal of the shortcomings of Bukharin's reformist policy. In China, also prior to collectivization, there was a tendency for local cadres to withdraw from the Party, attempt to become local social-economic notables, and influence Party policy and organizations in pursuit of personal-social interests (see T. P. Bernstein's excellent piece, "Problems of Village Leadership After Land Reform," *China Quarterly* 36 [October-December 1968], esp. the section on the "threat from below," pp. 1-23). In this connection, Ilya Harik's piece on Egypt is valuable ("The Single Party as a Subordinate Movement: The Case of Egypt," *World Politics* XXVI, 1 [October 1973]: 80-106). See his distinction between collaboration and mobilization movements.

[58]Massell, p. 83.

Massell related this observation to the segmentary character of social organization in the area, and went on to note that under the circumstances

> valued lines of kin could serve as vehicles to fill whatever gaps there were. In effect, it is probable that ANY locally respected and strategically connected patriarch . . . could step into the place of lost traditional leaders . . . . It is also likely that heads of extended families or their eldest sons were able to form new, informally operating communal councils as quickly as members of old ones were removed.[59]

Still, pointing to the weaknesses of a reformist political economy strategy is not the same as demonstrating the effectiveness of a revolutionary sociocultural strategy as a means of creating a type of class-based society. To that end we shall now examine collectivization in Romania, China, and the Soviet Union. This should allow us to scrutinize and develop our argument about Leninism's "ingenious error."

---

[59]*Ibid.*

V

COLLECTIVIZATION

It would be erroneous to say that students of Leninist regimes have neglected collectivization. Especially in recent years with the works of Lewin, Bernstein, Millar, and others, collectivization has received a good deal of sophisticated attention.[1] However, it would *not* be erroneous to say that students of Communist countries have given the greater part of their attention to industrialization, and that when collectivization has been studied, it has been from an economic- or political-control perspective.[2]

Our thesis is twofold: *collectivization may be the most distinctive feature of Leninist regime strategies*, and its significance rests as much and perhaps more in its *social* than its economic impact.

Expanding on this thesis: (1) The neglect of the social dimensions of collectivization is extraordinary. (2) The distinctiveness of Leninist strategy may lie in collectivization as a particular means of undermining the peasant extended household and village—not so much as work units or social references, but rather as units and models of social, economic, and political power. (3) The effectiveness of collectivization as an attack on the status character of social organization is integrally related to a comprehensive policy of industrialization and education. (4) The collective farm may be viewed as a major instance of the neo-traditional organization of Leninist regimes. (5) An argument about the significance of collectivization as

---

[1] See M. Lewin, *Russian Peasants and Soviet Power: A Study of Collectivization* (Evanston: Northwestern University Press, 1968); James R. Millar, ed. *The Soviet Rural Community* (Urbana: University of Illinois Press, 1971); references to Bernstein's works have already been made.

[2] See, for example, J. R. Millar and Alec Nove, "Was Stalin Really Necessary? A Debate on Collectivization," *Problems of Communism* XXV, 4 (July and August 1976): 49-63. Nove's argument is the more insightful.

a defining feature of Leninist strategy does not depend on every Leninist regime implementing collectivization with the same urgency or in the same fashion.

Fortunately, there are some studies of the social impact of collectivization that can be examined in terms of these arguments. We shall approach these studies with the following questions: Do they provide evidence that collectivization undermines the peasant-status quality of social and cultural life, favors the emergence of nuclear families and the individual over the peasant extended household, and not only supports but also entails the effective introduction of authoritative and superordinate impersonal norms of action and organization?

Several studies about the impact of collectivization have been undertaken in Romania. Without doubt the most valuable has been the Romanian rural sociologist Mihail Cernea's book *The Sociology of Collective Farms*. Cernea emphasizes that in *pre*-Communist Romania the family was the organizational matrix in both the social and economic realms. According to Cernea, commercialization and the consequent development of supra-and extra-familial associations did not remove the extended family as either the model of organization or as an integral component of socioeconomic (and political) organization and action.[3]

The centrality of the extended family household as the basic unit of identity and action in pre-Communist Romania also comes out quite clearly in Verdery's study of a Transylvanian village that had a German and Romanian population. She found that Germans and Romanians measured prestige in radically different ways. Germans "assessed one another's position by a set of ideas about *individual* character, capabilities, and personal traits. . . . Rich Germans whose character was found wanting were simply not esteemed." In contrast, the unit ranked by the Romanians was not the individual; it was the household.[4]

How did collectivization affect this situation? Cernea argues that collectivization has created new types of organization which are formal rather than social. It has removed "familialism" as the fundamental organizing principle of agricultural organization. The brigade and team replaced the peasant family as the basic work units. The brigade made the individual the core production unit and (to a

[3]Cernea, pp. 420-58.
[4]Verdery, pp. 256-57.

greater or lesser extent) detached him from his familial ties while subordinating him to non-familial hierarchies and authorities based on impersonal orientations. This substitution of formal organization based on impersonal norms and the individual for social organization based on personal norms and the extended household was reinforced by a new system of remuneration based on the *individual's* work day.[5] The brigade system, which operated for twenty years, can be seen as an assault on the status organization of the village and peasant extended household.

But how effective was the brigade system in Romania (or China and the Soviet Union?)—and what do we mean by effective? These questions are crucial in light of two phenomena: (a) in Communist countries the family's role as a locus of trust and a unit of mutual help and gain has in certain respects been reinforced;[6] and (b) in recent times the extended family has reappeared as the basic work unit in some collective farms. The meaning of these two phenomena is by no means self-evident. *Plus ça change, plus c'est la même chose* may appeal to some as a conclusion about social change under Leninist auspices. It certainly does not tax one intellectually or in many cases ideologically. But "economical" as such a conclusion might be, it is extremely misleading.

The discovery by some observers that the extended family is still a prominent feature of the Romanian (and Chinese) landscape is important but somewhat superficial. As a corrective to notions that social change can be conceived of in absolute terms, it is useful, but that is the extent of its usefulness. *The question is not whether the peasant extended patriarchal household has been completely eliminated, but whether it has maintained or lost its integrity as the institution providing personal identity, exercising social, economic, and political influence, and acting as the cultural model of authority and interpersonal relations.*

To observe that the peasant extended household still functions is not nearly as important as knowing *how* it functions and in what setting. To establish the meaning and significance of the extended family's continued presence in Communist countries like Romania

[5]Cernea, p. 199.

[6]In response to periods of terror and provocation, the family became in some respects even more closely bound. In this connection, see A. Inkeles and Raymond A. Bauer, *The Soviet Citizen* (Cambridge, Mass.: Harvard University Press, 1961), pp. 210-33, and H. Kent Geiger, *The Family in Soviet Russia* (Cambridge, Mass.: Harvard University Press, 1968), parts III, IV, and V.

and China, one must examine the present internal organization of the "extended" household, look at the political institutional context in which such a family operates, and identify the types of norms that effectively shape the behavior of its members. Viewed in this contextual light, Cole's findings in Romania and Parrish's in China have very different meanings from those the authors argue.

Cole's interesting discovery that the extended family still functions in the industrialized county of Brasov (Romania) does not present much of a challenge to our thesis that collectivization (*cum* industrialization and education) undermines the integrity of the peasant extended household.[7] Parrish has examined the impact of collectivization on the Chinese village. Among his conclusions are the following: the production team in the collective is "somewhat traditional/somewhat modern"; one of the reasons agricultural transformation was comparatively easy and rapid in the mid-1950's was that collectivization relied heavily on natural communities; there seem to have been shifts in social patterns in the countryside which in some ways made certain types of villages more "encysted" than they were even twenty years ago; new collectives and the subsequent brigade and team units tended simply to enclose old villages and surname groups.[8] Evidently, there is not much support here for the recasting or transformatory power of Leninist collectivization. However, Parrish has more to say about the Chinese village since collectivization. It seems that "today there is less need to mobilize *kinsmen* outside the village simply because the *cooperation of fellow villagers is guaranteed* by the collective interest everyone has in the success of the year's harvest. To an extent . . . the narrow administrative circle has replaced the wider network of kinship."[9]

Since collectivization the village may in certain respects be more self-contained, *but* not "encysted." Parrish's uses of the terms "narrow" and "wider" mislead as much as they inform. That village

---

[7] John Cole, "Familial Dynamics in a Romanian Worker Village," *Dialectical Anthropology* 1, 3 (May 1976): 251-67. My critique of Cole's conclusions is balanced by my appreciation of the very valuable empirical work he and his students are doing in Romania today.

[8] See William L. Parrish, "China—Team, Brigade, or Commune?," *Problems of Communism* XXV (March-April 1976): 51-66; also see the same author's "Socialism and the Chinese Peasant Family," *Journal of Asian Studies* XXXIV (May 1975): 613-30.

[9] Parrish, "China—Team, Brigade, or Commune?," p. 54.

COLLECTIVIZATION

neighbors rather than kin from several villages now cooperate economically may well signify a dramatic shift *and broadening* of social organization. The "narrowness" of kin cooperation has been broadened to include "strangers"—in this case village neighbors. In similar fashion, neighbors now marry inside the village rather than going outside, and villages have their own schools. What appears to Parrish to be a narrowing appears to me to be a broadening process, one that decompartmentalizes the status-kinship divisions in a corporate-familial society. Furthermore, that interactions between individuals at the higher commune level are more formal, impersonal, and limited in scope is not necessarily a weakness of the rural system. Insofar as this development entails the breakup of status familial organization at the level of the "standard marketing area" *without* removing the family as a source of private solidarity or work at various levels, it may in fact be an element of strength.[10]

The decisive change in China, Romania, the Soviet Union, and other Communist countries has been the imposition—in the rural as well as urban areas—of authoritative and effective frameworks of action and organization neither modeled after nor based on the extended family. This does not mean status practices and orientations have been eliminated; it means they have effectively and regularly been subordinated to the regime's formal institutions and goals. The critical issue is not whether one can find instances of nepotism, corruption, and familialism in Communist countries. It is whether these practices are informal responses in the context of authoritative institutions that limit their incidence and ensure to a great extent that they add to rather than take away from the regime's effective pursuit of its goals, or whether these practices are founded on largely intact status institutions that effectively compete with and subvert the operation of the regime's formal institutions and goals. *To date*, the difference between Leninist and Third World regimes is precisely in the greater success the former have had in subordinating status practices and orientations to the level of informal (not insignificant) behavior.[11]

[10]Insofar as a structurally multidimensional society is more adaptive than a society all of whose institutions and realms of social action are predicated on the same principle of orientation and organization.

[11]This achievement is subject to developmental challenges, some of which Leninist regimes may be *less* successful in handling. I speculate about one such challenge below in "Familialism in Communist Countries: A Conjecture" (see pp. 69-73).

To reiterate: the discovery of the continued existence of the extended family, the "narrowing" of the village, and corruption cannot be uncritically assumed to imply a lack of fundamental social change. One must ask: In what context do these practices and institutions exist, and consequently what systemic weight and character do they possess?

In his study of collectivization, Cernea notes the *reappearance of the family as a strategic work unit in the collective farm*. He goes on to ask the appropriate question: Does the reappearance of the family as the basic work unit in the collective farm mean the cooptation of the collective by the family? His answer is that the family unit has been incorporated at only one level of action—that of task execution. The system of *acord global*, one that recognizes the family as the contractual unit of work, utilizes "familialism" only where it proves functional—in work execution.[12] This functional recognition does not favor the reappearance of the (peasant) corporate patriarchal family as much as it favors an instrumentally oriented family made up of members with supplementary incomes and diverse careers, oriented as much to contracts as to connections and to individual interests as to corporate ones.

In fact, the reappearance of the family as an important unit in the Romanian collective farm is possible in good measure precisely because of the prior developmental phase during which the peasant extended household and village were *divested* of their model and power qualities. The family that currently participates in the Romanian *acord global*, the Russian "link" system, and the Chinese production team is not the family of pre-collectivization. *Collectivization has not eliminated the family; rather, in conjunction with education, industrialization, and Party organization, it has recast the family's internal definition and its place in the social system. Leninist regimes have transformed their societies to the point where phenomena that once were public are now primarily private in standing and character.* An example of this is Verdery's finding in the village collective she studied that former rich peasants and priests still receive *more* deference than either the Party secretary or the chairman of the collective.[13] *But* this deference has no direct political-economic significance. It is a private-social matter rather than (as in the past) an integral component and reflection of a particular type of social-political order.

[12]Cernea, pp. 208-209.
[13]Verdery, pp. 271 and 277.

There is further evidence of institutional change in the Soviet case. Ian Hill, in his judicious and valuable examination of the ways in which the Russian rural population *remains* peasant concludes with the following:

> Whilst, as I have indicated, certain groups still retain economic, social, and cultural peasant characteristics, in view of the depth and extent of cultural change it seems *doubtful whether these characteristics are sufficient for us to continue applying the term peasant to members of the rural population.* . . . The bulk of the rural population have learned to act within the confines of socialized agriculture and it seems that their peasant characteristics are a small element in their total cultural and behavioural makeup.[14]

Through the effective imposition of institutions (e. g., collective farms) which are neither modeled nor based primarily on personal norms of action and organization, and through the effective introduction of industrial and education policies, Leninist regimes have, to varying extents, successfully created societies *that allow greater social mobility for the individual and resource mobility for the regime.* They have created a neo-corporate variant of class society, a charismatic "substitute" for the procedural type of class society that developed in the West.

"FAMILIALISM" IN COMMUNIST COUNTRIES: A CONJECTURE

Though not to be understood as the persistence of the peasant corporate family, "familialism" may indeed be a current issue for Leninist regimes. *There may well be new forms of "familialism" in Communist countries, related to the routinization of the Party and the rationalization of society.*

As I stressed earlier, the auspices of social change shape the organization and meaning of change. To use a familiar example, the West did not simply experience industrialism and national development. Entrepreneurial capitalism and feudalism have given a particular cast to the pattern of economic, social, and political development in the West.

In Communist countries a charismatic political organization acting as the *purposive* and *dominant* agent of change has gener-

---

[14]Ian H. Hill, "The End of the Russian Peasantry?: The Social Structure and Culture of the Contemporary Soviet Agricultural Population," *Soviet Studies* 27, 1 (January 1975): 127.

ated a *neo-traditional ethos and institutional pattern at both the social and regime levels.* In Communist countries, status organization has not given way to the individual entrepreneur and citizen acting in market and public arenas. It has given way to a comprehensive set of neo-corporate institutions (e. g., unity fronts, official unions, collective farms) with official-political status. The deliberate preemption by the Party of any potential political arena or role not coterminous with its own organization and membership—i. e., *its collapsing of the official and political realms*—more than anything else determines the *character* of socio-political developments and the *manner* in which socio-political conflicts in Communist countries are manifested and resolved.

At the regime level the collapsing of the official and political realms favors *Party familialization*—i. e., the routinization of a charismatic organization in a traditional direction.[15] This tendency is not unprecedented in Leninist regimes. The "new class" phenomenon has been observed over and over again. *The difference today is the absence of a secret police-permanent purge mechanism able to ensure that the Party-apparatchik monopoly of political power does not become the monopoly of certain families who are in the Party.*

Viewed in this light, Khrushchev's attempts at educational reforms can be seen more *as attacks on the development of a ruling class of cadre families than as attacks on the development of a ruling class of Party cadres.*[16] Certainly Shirk's study of Chinese middle schools suggests that the children of cadres have many of the attitudes and styles one associates with an established elite of interconnected families, convinced of their "right to rule" and basing that conviction on ascriptive characteristics such as family origin and official position more than on achievement considerations.[17] In Romania, recent criticisms of Party cadres acting as baptismal sponsors in return for deference and material goods, as patrons of clients engaged in semi-legal and illegal business transactions ("*nasul afaceristilor*"), and as sponsors of (often unqualified) aspi-

---

[15]For Weber's comments on the traditionalization of charisma, see M. Weber, *Economy and Society*, vol. 1, pp. 246-54.

[16]See Jeremy Azrael, "Soviet Union," in *Education and Political Development*, ed. James S. Coleman (Princeton: Princeton University Press, 1965), pp. 233-72.

[17]Susan L. Shirk, "Schoolcraft in China: Political Culture as Strategic Behavior" (unpublished manuscript, 1977). I am most grateful to Professor Shirk for having sent me her article before its publication.

rants to Party or governmental offices point in the same direction.[18] Intermarriage at the Party elite level, "closing off" mobility at certain levels to non-elite families, and the development of a "right to rule" mentality within elite families (both Party and Party-connected) are phenomena that warrant empirical investigation in light of our conjecture about the direction *Party traditionalization* may be taking.

The tendency toward "Party familialization" at the regime level has a counterpart at the social level. There also one encounters a phenomenon that can be approached in terms of a "familialism" different in character from what existed prior to the developmental efforts of Leninist regimes.[19] The efforts have succeeded noticeably in changing the occupational and educational profiles of Communist countries. One striking manifestation is the emergence of a broad stratum oriented to achievement norms, calculable rules, and the nuclear family as the locus of affection and individual effort. *However, the ethos and orientation of this stratum has a distinctive cast*, one that often escapes those whose major interest is changes in social stratification. This ethos and orientation may be seen as a defensive response to the preemption of public political life by the Party-official stratum.

What one finds in Communist countries today in some ways fits as well as any nineteenth-century Western example the picture of bourgeois society Marx drew in "On the Jewish Question."[20] One can point to a growing stratum of families whose achievement orientations and emphasis on individual effort and responsibility are suffused with an overriding concern about private life, private gain, self-interest, and career advancement. The political manifestation of this "selfish" individualism is the highly instrumental conception of regime legitimacy one finds within this stratum.[21] *If we define as legitimate a regime able to assume the voluntary provision of private resources for official or public purposes*, then in basic (not

[18]See *Scinteia* (Bucharest) September 24, 1977, pp. 2-3.

[19]By "developmental efforts," I mean the collectivization, industrialization, and educational efforts of the Party.

[20]Karl Marx, "On the Jewish Question," in *The Marx-Engels Reader*, ed Robert C. Tucker (New York: W. W. Norton & Company, 1972), pp. 24-52.

[21]This observation is based on the author's experience and the observations of other students of Leninist regimes. Unfortunately, it does not have the support of survey data that would provide a more disaggregated and differentiated picture of political attitudes in these societies.

all) respects regimes in Communist countries are not very legitimate.[22] In some respects, Banfield's image of peasant amoral society can be transferred to Communist countries under the label of urban amoral society.[23]

Ironically, the tendency at the regime level toward routinization of a party based on charismatic impersonalism into a syncretic organizational-familial status group has been paralleled at the social level by the relative demise of status and the crystallization of a type of class orientation and family organization.

To be sure, this brief discussion of "familialism" at the regime and social levels in Communist countries is speculative and schematic—and deliberately so. The motive is to identify those sociopolitical tendencies likely to define the field within which all politically conflictual forces in these countries interact. Among these forces one should include the following: (1) the continued existence in Leninist regimes of leadership cadres committed to a conception of the Party as an heroic impersonal organization and opposed to its routinization into a syncretic organizational-familial status group; (2) the widespread existence and persistence of status-like attitudes among the peasantry, working class, and professional strata concerned with (job) security and maintenance of personal connections with those of elite status; and (3) the pressure on these regimes to respond positively to class-like developments in their own orders—pressures that come from increasing ties with Western economies and societies and that probably support those sectors within Leninist regimes more oriented to class than status or charismatic modes of action and organization.

An identification of contrasting regime and social developments is not a sufficient base for deducing the timing or specific content of particular crises, however. Nor can one deduce from a conceptual statement of this order—one that attempts to synthetically portray the distinctive quality of Leninist socio-political organization and analytically identify the basic conflict points in that organization—the inevitability of political "degeneration" or cata-

---

[22]This statement should not preclude an appreciation of the extent to which a given regime's legitimacy varies over time and with respect to *different* facets of national life—e. g., participation, national defense capacity, or social welfare measures.

[23]Edward C. Banfield, *The Moral Basis of a Backward Society* (New York: The Free Press, 1958), *passim.*

clysm. To deal with the timing and content of crises, the formulations offered here must be complemented by empirical studies of particular Leninist regimes.

My effort in this work has had a different purpose. I have tried to conceptually specify the novelty of Leninism as political organization and strategy. I have proceeded on the assumption that the meaning of organization, strategy, and conflict in Communist countries is not self-evident and that an adequate understanding of the developmental history and institutional profile of these regimes depends on more adequate conceptualization. Nowhere is this need more evident than in the relation between the national and international development of Leninist regimes.

VI

COMBINED SUBSTITUTION

Our analysis of Leninism as a particular response to the status organization of peasant society and the related phenomenon of dependency has been primarily national in focus.[1] The value of such a perspective, even if not fully realized in this piece, justifies such a study. However, simple observation strongly suggests that an historical and organizational phenomenon like the Soviet Bloc was an integral—not marginal—part of the Leninist "response." For practically all Leninist regimes, dependence on the Soviet Union has been a defining feature of their developmental efforts for a greater or lesser part of their existence. *The implication is that any attempt to specify the distinctiveness of Leninism as a response to the status organization of peasant society and dependency must include and explain the relationship between national and international levels of action and organization.* I shall attempt to do so in this chapter.

In addressing this task, I shall introduce the notion of "combined substitution"—a concept that speaks both to the distinctiveness of Leninism as a national/international response to dependency and to the general need for concepts that systematically relate the national and international dimensions of socio-political change.

So far, three features of Leninism as a novel and effective (if not highly efficient or legitimate)[2] mode of social change in a

---

[1] But not entirely so. I would like to think that the argument about the structural congruity between the ordering of international relations and the internal ordering of a status society speaks directly to the issue of linking national-international events (see pp. 24-29 above).

[2] To be useful, the notions of "efficient" and "legitimate" must be related to the central ideological and situational features of an elite and society that are involved in a revolutionary process. I have made some observations on the issue of legitimacy in a revolutionary situation in Jowitt, *Revolutionary Breakthroughs and National Development*, pp. 115-20. I shall expand on them in a monograph on *Developmental Tasks and Regime Structures in Communist Countries*.

peasant country have been identified: the substitution of charismatic for procedural impersonalism, the recasting of status and the development of class features under charismatic organizational auspices, and Leninism's "ingenious error" of analysis, with an accompanying emphasis on institutional, not just elite, transformation of the agrarian sector.

A glance at the international position of most Communist countries—at least during their initial phases of development—appears to seriously complicate this view, however. For a country like Romania (and in this case Romania typifies the greater number of Leninist regimes), one might argue that under the auspices of this novel Leninist organization, it simply shifted its "neocolonial" referent from France (or Germany) to the Soviet Union. In fact, "neocolonial" is too charitable a term. For more than a decade, most Communist countries were more colonies than neo-colonies of the Soviet Union. The presence of Soviet troops, advisers, secret police officials, economic plans establishing the priority of Soviet interests, and the imposition of Soviet political and economic models meant direct Soviet domination, with significant impact for a whole range of immediate and long-term conflicts, from intra- and inter-Party conflicts to issues of national legitimacy for each of these regimes. Important as this dimension of Soviet colonialism is, however, it in no way exhausts its sigificance, for in a major respect Soviet colonialism under Stalin was "colonialism of a new type."

For approximately a decade, the organization of the Soviet Bloc was strictly analogous to the organization of a Leninist party. The relationship between the Communist Party of the Soviet Union (CPSU) and non-Soviet ruling parties was based on status and class features recast and shaped by charismatic impersonalism. As for *status* features, just as a Leninist party is based on the neo-traditional insider-outsider distinction, so under the aegis of the Soviet Union, the Soviet Bloc was a political entity of insiders vs. outsiders. Just as each local party provided some sense of security for its members, so the Soviet regime provided political and military security for each of its member-regimes.[3] Just as each party was led by a figure readily intelligible in traditional terms (i. e., Mao Tse-tung, Tito, Gheorghiu-

---

[3]Furthermore, within the Bloc, as within each party, security was threatened by the leadership's peremptory-arbitrary actions (i. e., purges)—in the former by the Soviet leadership, in the latter by the leadership of each party vis-à-vis its internal membership.

Dej, Ho Chi Minh), so the regime Bloc was led by a "big man," Stalin, a leader whose heroic feats—collectivization, industrialization, and defeat of the Nazis—created awe and inspired the conviction that "socialism in one country" could be generalized outside the Soviet setting.

This conviction was underwritten by Soviet *insistence* that each Leninist regime could and must replicate the Soviet industrial-rural breakthrough. As Granick and even more so Shoup have argued, this insistence that the "colonies" engage in rapid and comprehensive industrialization and rural transformation was a unique form of colonialism.[4] This colonialism insisted on the creation of engineers and agronomists, the building of factories and heavy industry, and the creation of an educational network and opportunities for social mobility on a scale that no other modern form of colonialism has come close to matching. These priorities reflected the *class*-order commitments and goals of each Leninist regime and the superordinate Soviet regime. That they were conceived of and organized as a rapid, intense, and often irrational assault was due to the heroic-charismatic ethos and orientation of those regimes.[5] The Bloc was organized in the same terms and fashion as individual Leninist parties, *but it was an international unit*, and as such it added a crucial dimension to the efforts of its individual members to break through a "neocolonial"-dependency pattern.

To break through dependency in a peasant country, a political organization with a paradigm antithetical to that of a social order based on status must simultaneously insulate itself from and recast the institutions of a peasant society AND insulate the country itself from international ties that constrain, shape, and reinforce domestic institutional patterns.

I call the dual process of insulation-transformation at the

---

[4] See David Granick, "The Pattern of Foreign Trade in Eastern Europe and Its Relation to Economic Development Policy," *Quarterly Journal of Economics* LXVIII (August 1954): 377-401, and Paul Shoup, "Communism, Nationalism, and the Growth of the Communist Community of Nations After World War II," *American Political Science Review* 56 (December 1962): 886-98.

[5] One must be careful not to confuse the popular use of the terms "hero" and "heroism" with the concept of heroism. The former imply something good, a positively valued individual or action. The latter refers to a distinguishable type of behavior in which risk, prowess, and disdain for a rational calculus of cost and benefits are defining (though not the only) features.

national/international level combined substitution.[6] The Soviet Bloc in its initial phases is *one historical instance* of this phenomenon. *Under the aegis of the Soviet Union, the Bloc acted as an international organizational substitute* for the international membership and reference groupings that shaped elite self-conceptions in these countries before Leninist parties took power. While the local parties substituted domestically for the social elites and institutions of a peasant status society, the Soviet regime provided them the models, resources, resolution, and "space" to act on their shared programmatic-ideological commitments.

There are a number of things to be said about Leninism as an historical-organizational instance of combined substitution. First, we must come to grips with a fundamental distinction in the field of Communist studies between independent and "derivative" regimes. This distinction between regimes such as the Chinese and Bulgarian or Yugoslav and Romanian is accurate and useful—but not equally so for all questions.

While different countries and parties have had significantly different ties with the Soviet Union, and while these ties have changed significantly over time,[7] even independent regimes like the

---

[6]Combined substitution is an ideal-typical construct. Applied to the Soviet Bloc phenomenon, it selects and emphasizes the distinctive ideological and strategic tendencies and actions of Leninist elites organized in a particular national and international fashion. It is not an inexorable law, familiarity with which allows an analyst to ignore the level of contingent political action. The analyst must operate at two levels in order to explain particular developments. For example, the fact that in 1948 the Soviet Union called for the implementation of social transformation in Eastern Europe should not be seen as an automatic consequence of its ideological commitments and organizational character, but rather as the *coincidence of those two elements and the definition of its political interests in a particular set of environments (domestic, regional, international).* In a quite different setting, Outer Mongolia, social transformations were in good part put off by the Soviet Union for some thirty years; insulation was achieved, but transformation was in many respects delayed. The reasons for the delay are to be found at the level of political contingency—in this case, Soviet absorption in the 1930's, with its own social transformation and its concern over the role of Japan in Northeast Asia. *The critical link between the level of politically contingent actions and ideological-organizational imperatives is an elite's definition of political interests.* Presumably such definitions reflect ideological-organizational constants and environmental variables.

[7]I have tried to identify these changes in three works—K. Jowitt: "The Romanian Communist Party and the World Socialist System: A Redefinition of Unity," *World Politics* XXIII, 1 (October 1970): 38-61; "Inclusion and Mobiliza-

Chinese, Yugoslav, and Vietnamese have recognized an ideological, military, and/or organizational debt to the Soviet Union in their *initial efforts* to establish a new domestic and international position.[8] This observation should be seen as an addition, not an alternative, to the independent-derivative formulation. The conclusion to be drawn is that even the relationship between the independent regimes and the Soviet Union has been in certain important respects and at particular times *closer* than the typical relationship betweeen even allied sovereign states.

Second, there would appear to be a rather glaring anomaly to our argument that *combined substitution* is a necessary condition for avoiding or terminating a dependent domestic/international pattern. That anomaly is the Soviet case itself. The Soviet Union developed without the aid of a "bloc" substitute acting at the international level. Furthermore, of course, there are striking instances of non-Leninist countries avoiding dependency. In the nineteenth century, Japan and the United States provide two examples, as does Israel in the twentieth. All three underline a very important point—namely, while the Soviet Bloc postwar pattern is an extremely important historical instance of *combined substitution*, it should not be confused with the concept itself.

The exhaustion of the West after World War I, the potential within the Soviet Union to build "socialism in one country," and the initial and sustaining faith in revolutionary support from Western Europe are the components of the Soviet pattern of *combined substitution*. In the American case, the de facto international insulation provided by the British Navy and the absence of a peasantry domestically is another instance of combined substitution. I am not familiar with the Japanese case, but surely the role of the British Empire in the nineteenth century and the peculiar social-organizational domestic order that Nakane has so insightfully described are central to Japan's avoidance of dependency. What distinguishes the Soviet Bloc pattern (not to be confused with the Soviet case per se) as an instance of *combined substitution* is that a set of countries trans-

---

tion in European Leninist Systems," *World Politics* XXVIII 1 (October 1975): 69-97; and *Images of Détente and the Soviet Political Order* (Berkeley: Institute of International Studies, 1977) [Policy Papers in International Affairs, No. 1].

[8] At later dates these and other Leninist regimes have emphasized the negative contributions of the Soviet regime and their own "self reliance"; while significant for the analyst, such declarations should not be viewed uncritically.

formed their domestic social order and international position *under the deliberate organizational auspices of a great power with whom they shared an ideological affinity.*

As our limited discussion has already suggested, the particular Soviet Bloc pattern of combined substitution is not the only one that has historically "worked." *But* it is worth noting that the domestic and international situation of most contemporary Third World peasant countries attempting to create sovereign national and modern social orders is closer to that of prewar Romania or Bulgaria than to the United States or Japan in the nineteenth century or the Soviet Union or Israel in the twentieth. Regardless of what similarities there may be, however, the particular Leninist pattern of *combined substitution* that was applied to the postwar period is no longer available to most of the Third World for the following reasons. First, there is no single leader in the Soviet Bloc able to elicit the kind of awe and exercise the kind of power-authority that Stalin could. Second, Soviet Leninism, which after World War I was viewed by some activists in the colonies as revolutionary and liberating, is now seen by many as the conservative system of a powerful and potentially threatening state—the Soviet Union. Third, the emphasis (misplaced to an extent, if this analysis is correct) contemporary Third World regimes place on national "self-reliance" works against the creation of a bloc comparable to the Soviet postwar phenomenon.

For all these reasons, I suggest that Leninism is best seen as an *historical* as well as organizational syndrome, consisting of a political *organization* based on charismatic impersonalism, a *strategy* based on an "ingenious error" leading to collectivization-industrialization, and an international Bloc led by a dominant regime, with the same definition as its constituent parts, acting as leader, model, and support. In this light, the Cuban revolution and Cuba's relationship to the Soviet Union are watershed events that call for careful examination and formulation.

One of the more intriguing questions of the latter part of the twentieth century is whether new combined substitution patterns of national development will emerge in the Third World or elsewhere.

BIBLIOGRAPHY

Azrael, Jeremy. "Soviet Union." In *Education and Political Development*, ed. James S. Coleman. Princeton: Princeton University Press, 1965, pp. 233-72.

Bates, Robert H. *Rural Responses to Industrialization: A Study of Village Zambia.* New Haven: Yale University Press, 1976.

Beaber, Lawrence R. "Austria and the Emergence of Rumania, 1855-1861," *East European Quarterly* XI (Spring 1977): 65-78.

Bell, John D. *Peasants in Power: Alexander Stamboliiski and the Bulgarian Agrarian National Union: 1899-1923.* Princeton: Princeton University Press, 1977.

Berg, Elliot J. "Socialism and Economic Development in Tropical Africa," *Quarterly Journal of Economics* LXXVIII (November 1964): 549-74.

Bernstein, Thomas P. "Leadership and Mass Mobilization in the Soviet and Chinese Collectivization Campaigns of 1929-1930 and 1955-1956: A Comparison," *China Quarterly* 31 (July-September 1967): 1-47.

_____. "Problems of Village Leadership After Land Reform," *China Quarterly* 36 (October-December 1968).

Breslauer, George. "Khrushchev Reconsidered," *Problems of Communism* XXV, 5 (September-October 1976): 18-34.

Brzezinski, Zbigniew. "Conclusion: The African Challenge." In *Africa and the Communist World*, ed. Z. Brzezinski. Stanford: Stanford University Press, 1965.

_____. "The Soviet Political System: Transformation or Degeneration?" In *Dilemmas of Change in Soviet Politics*, ed. Z. Brzezinski. New York: Columbia University Press, 1969, pp. 1-35.

Cernea, Mihail. *Sociologia cooperativei agricole de producţie* [The sociology of collective farms]. Bucharest, 1974.

Cole, John. "Familial Dynamics in a Romanian Worker Village," *Dialectical Anthropology* 1, 3 (May 1976): 251-67.

Connor, W. Robert. *The New Politicians of Fifth Century Athens.* Princeton: Princeton University Press, 1971.

Dahrendorf, Ralf. *Society and Democracy in Germany.* New York: Doubleday, 1967.

Deutsch, Karl. "Social Mobilization and Political Development," *American Political Science Review* LV, 3 (September 1961): 493-514.

BIBLIOGRAPHY

Dobrogeanu-Gherea, Constantin. *Neoiobăgia*. Bucharest: Editura Librăriei SOCEC & Comp., 1910.

———. "Anarhia Cugetarii." in C. Dobrogeanu-Gherea, *Scrieri social-politice*. Bucharest: Editura Politică, 1968.

———. "Post-scriptum sau cuvinte uitate." In C. Dobrogeanu-Gherea, *Scrieri social-politice*. Bucharest: Editura Politică, 1968.

———. "Socialismul in Romania." In C. Dobrogeanu-Gherea, *Scrieri social-politice*. Bucharest: Editura Politică, 1968.

Ekeh, Peter." Colonialism and the Two Publics in Africa: A Theoretical Statement," *Comparative Studies in Society and History* 17 (January 1975): 91-112.

Fainsod, Merle. *Smolensk Under Soviet Rule*. New York: Vintage Russian Library, 1958.

Fall, Bernard B., ed. *Ho Chi Minh On Revolution: Selected Writings, 1920-66*. New York: Praeger, 1967.

Fanon, Frantz. *The Wretched of the Earth*. New York: Grove Press, 1966.

Foster, George. "Peasant Society and the Image of Limited Good," *American Anthropologist* 65 (April 1965): 293-315.

Geiger, H. Kent. *The Family in Soviet Russia*. Cambridge, Mass.: Harvard University Press, 1968.

Gerschenkron, Alexander. "The Approach to European Industrialization: A Postscript." In A. Gerschenkron, *Economic Backwardness in Historical Perspective*. Cambridge, Mass.: Harvard University Press, 1966, pp. 353-67.

———. "Economic Backwardness in Historical Perspective." In A. Gerschenkron, *Economic Backwardness in Historical Perspective*. Cambridge, Mass.: Harvard University Press, 1966.

Gonzalez, Edward. *Cuba Under Castro: The Limits of Charisma*. Boston: Houghton-Mifflin, 1974.

Granick, David. "The Pattern of Foreign Trade in Eastern Europe and Its Relation to Economic Development Policy," *Quarterly Journal of Economics* LXVIII (August 1954): 377-401.

Green, Reginald Herbold. "Political Independence and the National Economy: An Essay on the Political Economy of Decolonisation." In *African Perspectives*, eds. Christopher Allen and R. W. Johnson. Cambridge: Cambridge University Press, 1970, pp. 273-325.

Harik, Ilya. "The Single Party as a Subordinate Movement: The Case of Egypt," *World Politics* XXVI, 1 (October 1973): 80-106.

Hartz, Louis. *The Liberal Tradition in America*. New York: Harcourt, Brace & World, 1955.

Hill, Frances. "Ujamaa: African Socialist Productionism in Tanzania." In *Socialism in the Third World*, eds. Helen Desfosses and Jacques Levesque. New York: Praeger, 1975, pp. 216-55.

THE LENINIST RESPONSE TO NATIONAL DEPENDENCY

Hill, Ian H. "The End of the Russian Peasantry?: The Social Structure and Culture of the Contemporary Soviet Agricultural Population," *Soviet Studies* 27, 1 (January 1975).

Huntington, Samuel P. "Social and Institutional Dynamics of One-Party Systems." In *Authoritarian Politics in Modern Society*, eds. S. P. Huntington and Clement H. Moore. New York: Basic Books, 1970, pp. 3-48.

The Iliad of Homer. Trans. Richard Lattimore. Chicago: University of Chicago Press, 1957.

Inkeles, Alex. *Becoming Modern*. Cambridge, Mass.: Harvard University Press, 1974.

_____, and Bauer, Raymond A. *The Soviet Citizen*. Cambridge, Mass.: Harvard University Press, 1961.

Janos, Andrew. "The Decline of Oligarchy: Bureaucratic and Mass Politics in the Age of Dualism (1867-1918)." In *Revolution in Perspective: Essays on the Hungarian Soviet Republic*, eds. A. C. Janos and William B. Slottman. Berkeley: University of California Press, 1971, pp. 1-61.

Johnson, Chalmers A. *Peasant Nationalism and Communist Power*. Stanford: Stanford University Press, 1962.

_____. "Peasant Nationalism Revisited: The Biography of a Book," *China Quarterly*, December 1977.

Jowitt, Kenneth. *Images of Détente and the Soviet Political Order*. Berkeley: Institute of International Studies, University of California, 1977. [Policy Papers in International Affairs, No. 1]

_____. *Revolutionary Breakthroughs and National Development*. Berkeley: University of California Press, 1971.

_____. "Inclusion and Mobilization in European Leninist Regimes," *World Politics* XXVIII, 1 (October 1975): 69-97.

_____. "An Organizational Approach to the Study of Political Culture in Marxist-Leninist Systems," *American Political Science Review* LXVIII, 3 (September 1974): 1171-91.

_____. "The Romanian Communist Party and the World Socialist System: A Redefinition of Unity," *World Politics* XXIII, 1 (October 1970): 38-61.

Lattimore, Owen. *Nationalism and Revolution in Mongolia*. New York: Oxford University Press, 1955.

Lenin, V. I. "Left-Wing Communism—An Infantile Disorder," in V. I. Lenin, *Collected Works*, vol. 31 (April-December 1920). Moscow: Progress Publishers, 1966.

Lewin, M. *Russian Peasants and Soviet Power: A Study of Collectivization*. Evanston, Ill.: Northwestern University Press, 1968.

Leys, Colin. *Underdevelopment in Kenya: The Political Economy of Neo-Colonialism*. Berkeley and Los Angeles: University of California Press, 1974.

BIBLIOGRAPHY

Lovinescu, Eugen. *Istoria civilizaţiei Române moderne*. Bucharest: Editura Stiinţifică, 1972.

Lowenthal, Richard. "Development vs. Utopia in Communist Policy." In *Change in Communist Systems*, ed. Chalmers Johnson. Stanford: Stanford University Press, 1970, pp. 33-117.

Madgearu, Virgil. *Agrarianism, Capitalism, şi Imperialism*. Bucharest: Editura "Economistul," 1936.

Marx, Karl. "On the Jewish Question." In *The Marx-Engels Reader*, ed. Robert C. Tucker. New York: W. W. Norton, 1972, pp. 24-52.

Massell, Gregory. *The Surrogate Proletariat*. Princeton: Princeton University Press, 1974.

Mauss, Marcel. *The Gift*. New York: W. W. Norton, 1967.

Millar, James R., ed. *The Soviet Rural Community*. Urbana: University of Illinois Press, 1971.

_____, and Nove, Alec. "Was Stalin Really Necessary? A Debate on Collectivization," *Problems of Communism* XXV, 4 (July-August 1976): 49-63.

Mitrany, David. *Marx Against the Peasant: A Study in Social Dogmatism*. New York: Collier Books, 1961.

Morse, Richard. "The Heritage of Latin America." In *The Founding of New Societies*, ed. Louis Hartz. New York: Harcourt, Brace & World, 1964, pp. 123-78.

Nyomarkey, Joseph. "Factionalism in the National Socialist German Workers' Party, 1925-1926: The Myth and Reality of the 'Northern Faction,'" *Political Science Quarterly* LXXX, 1 (March 1965).

Obelkevich, James. *Religion and Rural Society: South Lindsey 1825-1875*. Oxford: Clarendon Press, 1976.

O'Brien, Donal B. Cruise. *Saints and Politicians*. New York: Cambridge University Press, 1975.

Parrish, William L. "China—Team, Brigade, or Commune?," *Problems of Communism* XXV (March-April 1976): 51-66.

_____. "Socialism and the Chinese Peasant Family," *Journal of Asian Studies* XXXIV (May 1975): pp. 613-30.

Pethybridge, Roger. *The Social Prelude to Stalinism*. London: Macmillan, 1974.

Polyani, Karl. *The Great Transformation*. Boston: Beacon Press, 1965.

Price, Robert. "Politics and Culture in Contemporary Ghana: The Big Man-Small Boy Syndrome," *Journal of African Studies* 1, 2 (Summer 1974): 173-204.

_____. "A Theoretical Approach to Military Rule in New States: Reference Group Theory and the Ghanaian Case," *World Politics* XXIII, 3 (April 1971): 399-430.

Pye, Lucian. *Guerilla Communism in Malaya.* Princeton: Princeton University Press, 1956.

Radulescu-Motru, C. *Cultura româna și politicianismul.* Bucharest, 1936.

Riggs, Fred W. "The Theory of Developing Polities." In F. Riggs, *Administration in Developing Countries.* Boston: Houghton-Mifflin, 1964, pp. 449-67.

Rothschild, Joseph. *The Communist Party of Bulgaria.* New York: Columbia University Press, 1959.

_____. *East Central Europe Between the Two World Wars.* Seattle and London: University of Washington Press, 1974.

Roberts, Henry. *Rumania: Political Problems of an Agrarian State.* New Haven: Yale University Press, 1951.

Rustow, Dankwart A. *A World of Nations.* Washington, D. C.: The Brookings Institution, 1967.

Saul, John. "African Socialism in One Country: Tanzania." In *Essays on the Political Economy of Africa*, eds. Giovanni Arrighi and J. S. Saul. New York: Monthly Review Press, 1973, pp. 237-336.

Schonfield, Hugh J. *The Pentecost Revolution.* London: Macdonald and Jane's St. Giles House, 1974.

Schumpeter, Joseph A. *Capitalism, Socialism and Democracy.* New York: Harper & Row, 1962.

Shanin, Teodor. *The Awkward Class.* Oxford: Clarendon Press, 1972.

Shirk, Susan L. "Schoolcraft in China: Political Culture as Strategic Behavior." Unpublished manuscript, 1977.

Shivji, Issa G. *Class Struggles in Tanzania.* New York: Monthly Review Press, 1976.

Shoup, Paul. "Communism, Nationalism, and the Growth of the Communist Community of Nations After World War II," *American Political Science Review* 56 (December 1962): 886-98.

Stalin, J. V. "Political Report of the Central Committee to the Sixteenth Congress of the Communist Party of the Soviet Union (Bolshevik), June 27, 1930." In J. V. Stalin, *Works*, vol. 12 (April 1929-June 1930). Moscow: Foreign Languages Publishing House, 1955; reprinted by Red Star Press, London, n. d.

_____. "Report to the Eighteenth Congress of the Communist Party of the Soviet Union (Bolshevik) on the Work of the Central Committee." In *The Essential Stalin*, ed. Bruce Franklin. Garden City, N. Y.: Doubleday, 1972.

Stavrianos, L. S. "The Influence of the West on the Balkans." In *The Balkans in Transition*, eds. Charles and Barbara Jelavich. Berkeley: University of California Press, 1963.

Stern, Fritz. *Gold and Iron: Bismarck, Bleichröder, and the Building of the German Empire.* New York: Alfred A. Knopf, 1977.

BIBLIOGRAPHY

Tucker, Robert C. *The Marxian Revolutionary Idea.* New York: W. W. Norton, 1969.

_____, ed. *The Lenin Anthology.* New York: W. W. Norton, 1975.

Turner, Henry Ashby, Jr. "Fascism and Modernization," *World Politics* XXIV, 4 (July 1972): 547-64.

Verdery, Katherine. "Ethnic Stratification in the European Periphery: The Historical Sociology of a Transylvanian Village." Ph.D. dissertation, Department of Anthropology, Stanford University, December 1976.

Vogel, Ezra. "From Friendship to Comradeship: The Change in Personal Relations in Communist China," *China Quarterly*, no. 2 (January-March 1965): 1-28.

Voinea, Şerban. *Marxism oligarhic.* Bucharest: Editura I. Brănişteanu, 1926.

Weber, Eugen. *Peasants into Frenchmen.* Stanford: Stanford University Press, 1976.

_____. "The Men of the Archangel," *Journal of Contemporary History* 1, 1 (1966): 101-27.

_____. "Romania." In *The European Right*, eds. Hans Rogger and E. Weber. Berkeley: University of California Press, 1966, pp. 501-75.

Weber, Max. *Economy and Society.* New York: Bedminster Press, 1968.

_____. *General Economic History.* Glencoe, Ill.: The Free Press, 1950.

_____. *The Protestant Ethic and the Spirit of Capitalism.* New York: Charles Scribner's Sons, 1958.

Weiss, Herbert. *Political Protest in the Congo.* Princeton: Princeton University Press, 1967.

Wilson, Edmund. *To the Finland Station.* Garden City, N. Y.: Doubleday, 1953.

Zeletin, Ştefan. *Burghezia română.* Bucharest: Cultura Natională, 1925.

About the author

Kenneth Jowitt is Associate Professor of Political Science at the University of California, Berkeley. His major interests are in the fields of comparative/international politics. He has published works on political organization and development in Communist countries, strategies of national development, the international organization of Communist regimes, and is currently working on the issue of political membership in industrial and non-industrial societies.

INSTITUTE OF INTERNATIONAL STUDIES
UNIVERSITY OF CALIFORNIA, BERKELEY

CARL G. ROSBERG,
Director

Monographs published by the Institute include:

RESEARCH SERIES

1. *The Chinese Anarchist Movement*, by Robert A. Scalapino and George T. Yu. ($1.00)
6. *Local Taxation in Tanganyika*, by Eugene C. Lee. ($1.00)
7. *Birth Rates in Latin America: New Estimates of Historical Trends*, by O. Andrew Collver. ($2.50)
12. *Land Tenure and Taxation in Nepal*, Volume IV, *Religious and Charitable Land Endowments: Guthi Tenure*, by Mahesh C. Regmi. ($2.75)
13. *The Pink Yo-Yo: Occupational Mobility in Belgrade, ca 1915-1965*, by Eugene A. Hammel. ($2.00)
14. *Community Development in Israel and the Netherlands: A Comparative Analysis*, by Ralph M. Kramer. ($2.50)
*15. *Central American Economic Integration: The Politics of Unequal Benefits*, by Stuart I. Fagan. ($2.00)
16. *The International Imperatives of Technology: Technological Development and the International Political System*, by Eugene B. Skolnikoff. ($2.95)
*17. *Autonomy or Dependence as Regional Integration Outcomes: Central America*, by Philippe C. Schmitter. ($1.75)
18. *Framework for a General Theory of Cognition and Choice*, by R.M. Axelrod. ($1.50)
19. *Entry of New Competitors in Yugoslav Market Socialism*, by S.R. Sacks. ($2.50)
*20. *Political Integration in French-Speaking Africa*, by Abdul A. Jalloh. ($3.50)
21. *The Desert and the Sown: Nomads in the Wider Society*, ed. by Cynthia Nelson. ($3.50)
22. *U.S.-Japanese Competition in International Markets: A Study of the Trade-Investment Cycle in Modern Capitalism*, by John E. Roemer. ($3.95)
23. *Political Disaffection Among British University Students: Concepts, Measurement, and Causes*, by Jack Citrin and David J. Elkins. ($2.00)
24. *Urban Inequality and Housing Policy in Tanzania: The Problem of Squatting*, by Richard E. Stren. ($2.50)
*25. *The Obsolescence of Regional Integration Theory*, by Ernst B. Haas. ($2.95)
26. *The Voluntary Service Agency in Israel*, by Ralph M. Kramer. ($2.00)
27. *The SOCSIM Demographic-Sociological Microsimulation Program: Operating Manual*, by Eugene A. Hammel et al. ($4.50)
28. *Authoritarian Politics in Communist Europe: Uniformity & Diversity in One-Party States*, ed. by Andrew C. Janos. ($3.95)
29. *The Anglo-Icelandic Cod War of 1972-1973: A Case Study of a Fishery Dispute*, by Jeffrey A. Hart. ($2.00)
30. *Plural Societies and New States: A Conceptual Analysis*, by Robert Jackson. ($2.00)
31. *The Politics of Crude Oil Pricing in the Middle East, 1970-1975: A Study in International Bargaining*, by Richard Chadbourn Weisberg. ($3.95)
32. *Agricultural Policy and Performance in Zambia: History, Prospects, and Proposals for Change*, by Doris Jansen Dodge. ($4.95)
33. *Five Classy Programs: Computer Procedures for the Classification of Households*, by E.A. Hammel and R.Z. Deuel. ($3.75)
34. *Housing the Urban Poor in Africa: Policy, Politics, and Bureaucracy in Mombasa*, by Richard E. Stren. ($5.95)
35. *The Russian New Right: Right-Wing Ideologies in the Contemporary USSR*, by Alexander Yanov. ($4.50)

*International Integration Series

INSTITUTE OF INTERNATIONAL STUDIES MONOGRAPHS (continued)

36. *Social Change in Romania, 1860-1940: A Debate on Development in a European Nation*, ed. by Kenneth Jowitt. ($4.50)
37. *The Leninist Response to National Dependency*, by Kenneth Jowitt. ($3.25)
38. *Socialism in Sub-Saharan Africa: A New Assessment*, ed. by Carl G. Rosberg and Thomas M. Callaghy. ($9.50)
39. *Tanzania's Ujamaa Villages: The Implementation of a Rural Development Strategy*, by Dean E. McHenry, Jr. ($5.95)
40. *Who Gains from Deep Ocean Mining? Simulating the Impact of Regimes for Regulating Nodule Exploitation*, by I.G. Bulkley. ($3.50)
41. *Industrialization, Industrialists, and the Nation-State in Peru: A Comparative/Sociological Analysis*, by Frits Wils. ($5.95)
42. *Ideology, Public Opinion, and Welfare Policy: Attitudes toward Taxes and Spending in Industrialized Societies*, by Richard M. Coughlin. ($4.95)
43. *The Apartheid Regime: Political Power and Racial Domination*, ed. by Robert M. Price and Carl G. Rosberg. ($8.95)
44. *The Yugoslav Economic System and Its Performance in the 1970s*, by Laura D'Andrea Tyson. ($4.50)

POLITICS OF MODERNIZATION SERIES

1. *Spanish Bureaucratic-Patrimonialism in America*, by Magali Sarfatti. ($2.00)
2. *Civil-Military Relations in Argentina, Chile, and Peru*, by Liisa North. ($2.00)
3. *Notes on the Process of Industrialization in Argentina, Chile, and Peru*, by Alcira Leiserson. ($1.75)
6. *Modernization and Coercion*, by Mario Barrera. ($1.50)
8. *Developmental Processes in Chilean Local Government*, by Peter S. Cleaves. ($1.50)
9. *Modernization and Bureaucratic-Authoritarianism: Studies in South American Politics*, by Guillermo A. O'Donnell. ($5.50)

POLICY PAPERS IN INTERNATIONAL AFFAIRS

1. *Images of Detente and the Soviet Political Order*, by Kenneth Jowitt. ($1.25)
2. *Detente After Brezhnev: The Domestic Roots of Soviet Foreign Policy*, by Alexander Yanov. ($3.00)
3. *The Mature Neighbor Policy: A New United States Economic Policy for Latin America*, by Albert Fishlow. ($2.00)
4. *Five Images of the Soviet Future: A Critical Review and Synthesis*, by George W. Breslauer. ($2.50)
5. *Global Evangelism Rides Again: How to Protect Human Rights Without Really Trying*, by Ernst B. Haas. ($2.00)
6. *Israel and Jordan: Implications of an Adversarial Partnership*, by I. Lustick ($2.00)
7. *Political Syncretism in Italy: Historical Coalition Strategies and the Present Crisis*, by Giuseppe Di Palma. ($2.00)
8. *U.S. Foreign Policy in Sub-Saharan Africa: National Interest and Global Strategy*, by Robert M. Price. ($2.25)
9. *East-West Technology Transfer in Perspective*, by R.J. Carrick. ($2.75)
10. *NATO's Unremarked Demise*, by Earl C. Ravenal. ($2.00)
11. *Toward an Africanized U.S. Policy for Southern Africa: A Strategy for Increasing Political Leverage*, by Ronald T. Libby. ($3.95)
12. *The Taiwan Relations Act and the Defense of the Republic of China*, by Edwin K. Snyder et al. ($3.95)
13. *Cuba's Policy in Africa, 1959-1980*, by William M. LeoGrande. ($3.25)

Address correspondence to:
Institute of International Studies
215 Moses Hall
University of California
Berkeley, California 94720

LIBRARY OF DAVIDSON COLLEGE

Books on regular loan may be checked   ooks